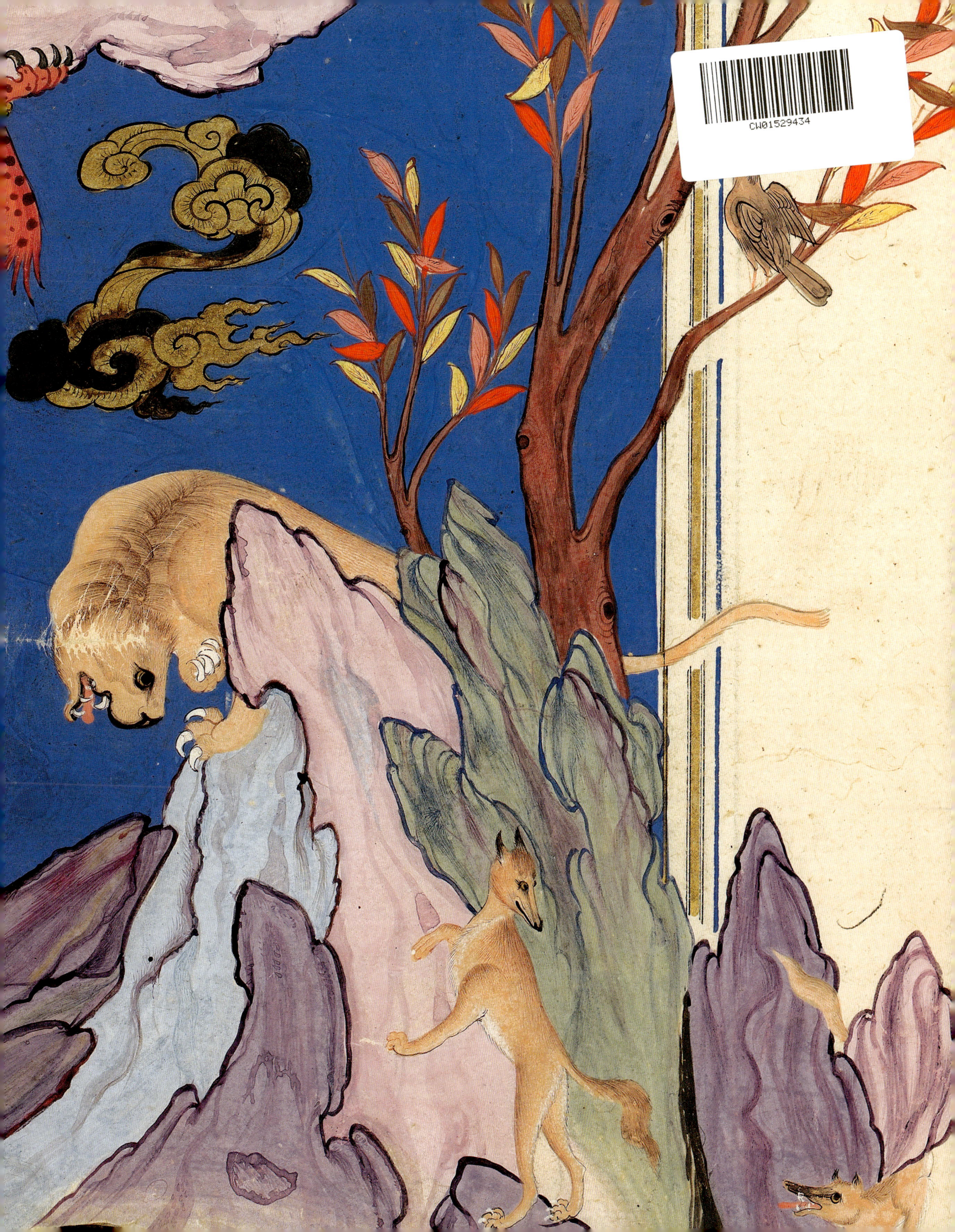

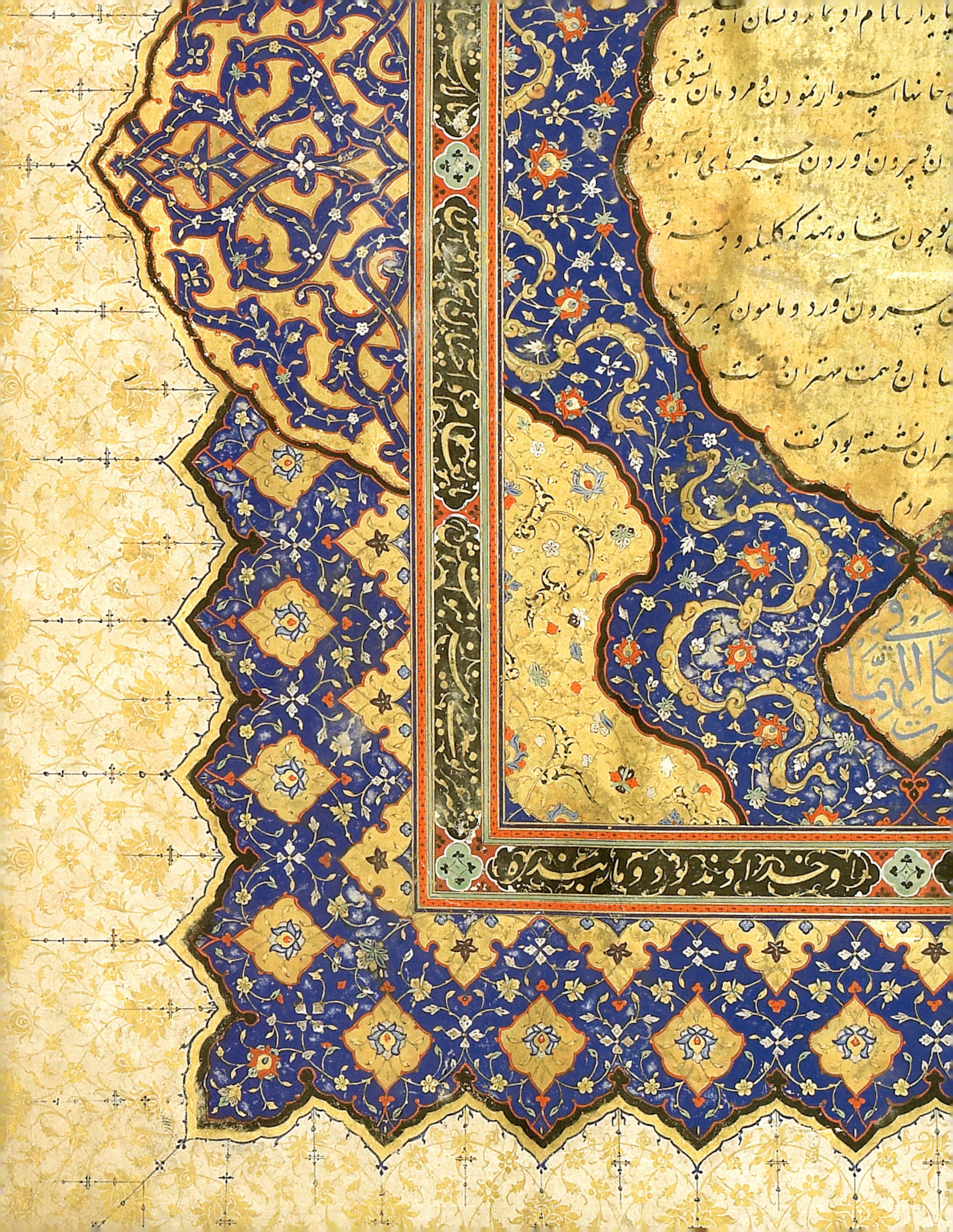

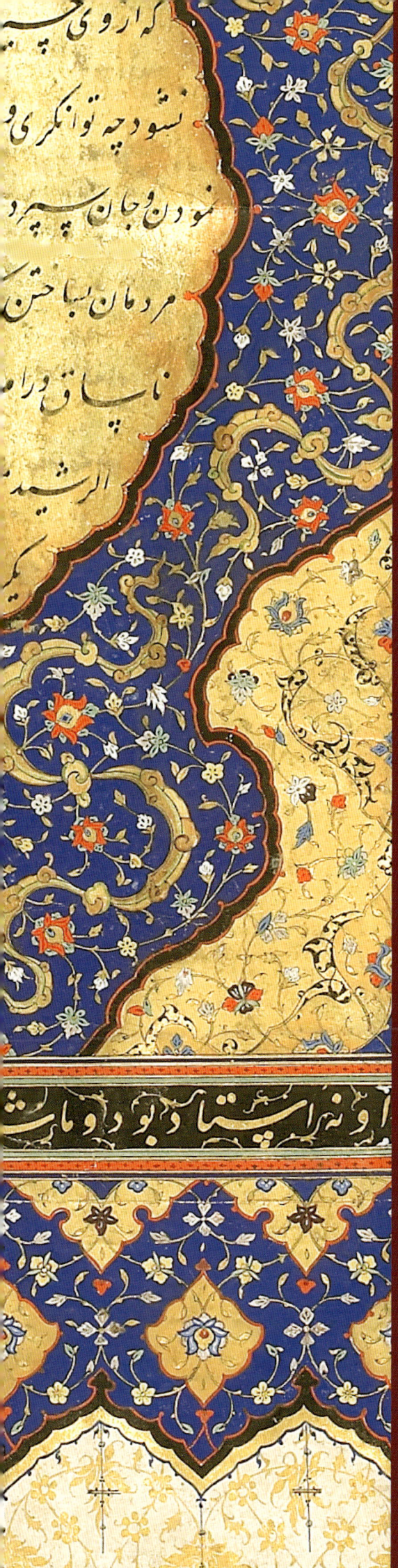

The Eckstein Shahnama
an Ottoman Book of Kings

WILL KWIATKOWSKI

SAM FOGG
15d Clifford Street
London W1S 4JZ

TEL. 020 7534 2100
FAX 020 7534 2122
EMAIL info@samfogg.com
WEBSITE www.samfogg.com

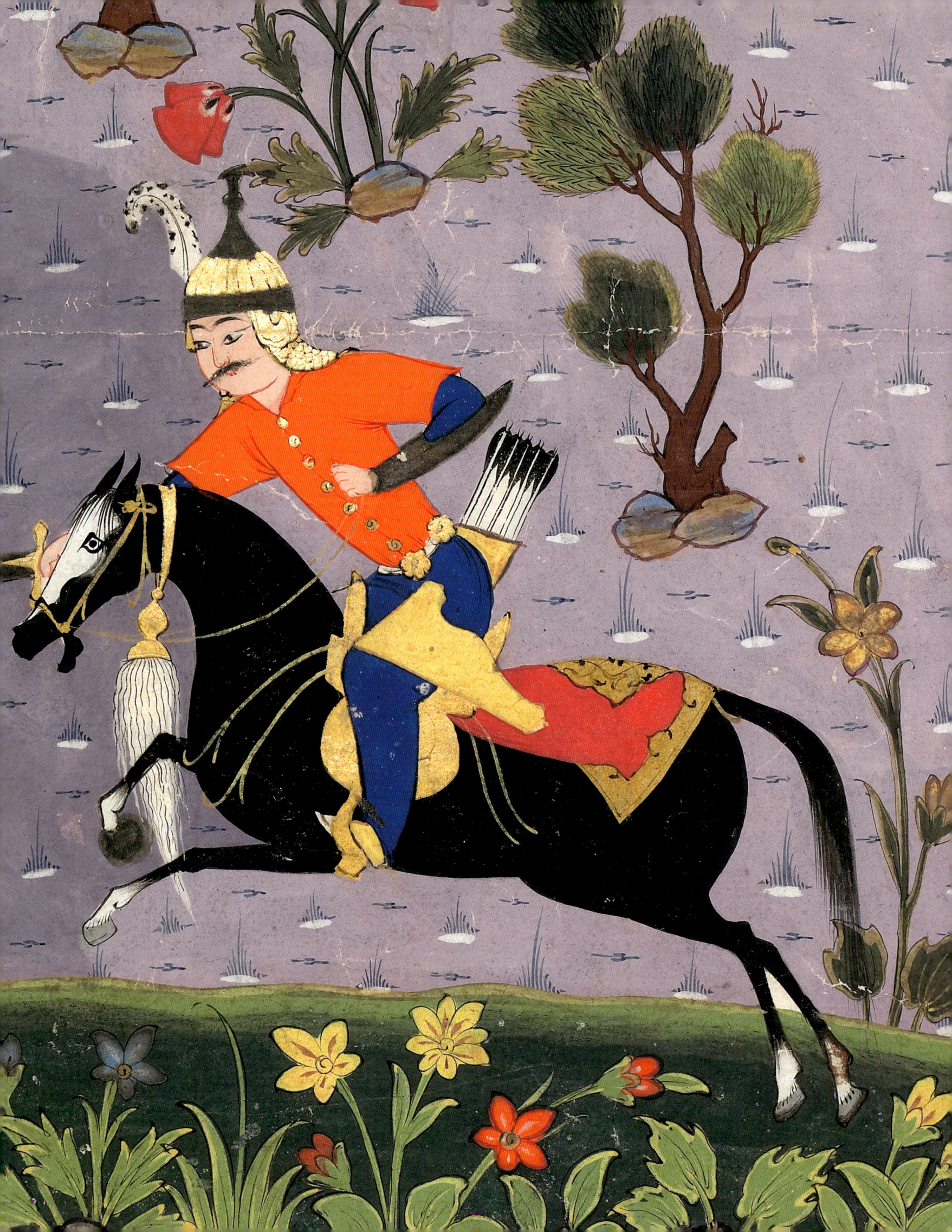

Contents

Introduction 7

The Manuscript

Description of the Manuscript 11

Colophons and Later Provenance 11

The Binding 12

The Organization of the Manuscript 13
I The truncated *Shahnamas* 13
II The preface 13
III The division of the manuscript 18
IV The headings 20

The Illumination 24

The Paintings 28

The Styles 32
I The first style (paintings nos. 1, 13, 18, 20–32) 32
II The second style (paintings nos. 2–4, 6–7, 9–12, 14–15, 17, 19) 41
III Other styles (paintings nos. 5, 8, 16) 44

The Detached Paintings 47

Analysis

The Eckstein *Shahnama* and Ottoman Ideology 51

The Eckstein *Shahnama* between Qazvin and the Ottoman Empire 54

Conclusion 59

Bibliography 64
Acknowledgements 64
Colophon 64

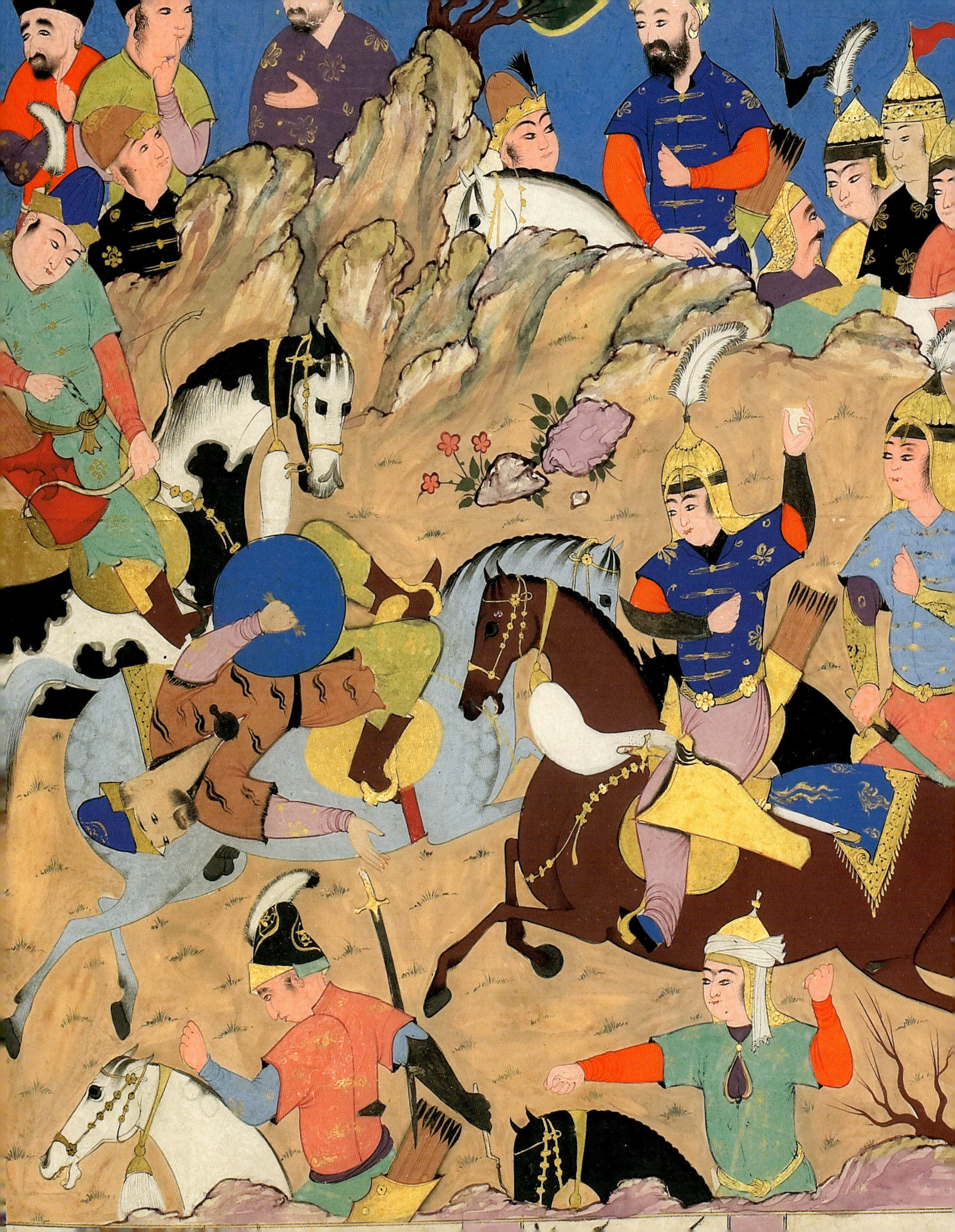

Introduction

No other work from the Persian literary canon rivals Firdausi's *Shahnama* as a celebration of Iran's ancient past. Written at the turn of the eleventh century CE, this poem of some 50,000 verses relates the history of Iran from the time of the first man and King of Iran, Gayumarth, down to the Arab conquests of the Near East and western Asia in the seventh century. Though often divided into 'mythical' and 'historical' sections, the poem actually consists of a seamless tapestry of historical and legendary material, in which battles with the foes of Iran and individual struggles with fierce demons and enemy champions are prominent.

The *Shahnama*, or 'Book of Kings', is also the most potent record of Iran's ancient tradition of kingship. In the *Shahnama* the reigns of the kings of Iran form not only the backbone of the narrative, but also the single greatest source of continuity in Iranian history. The murder of the last Sasanian king, Yazdagird, as he flees from the invading Arab army, marks not only the end of the narrative, but also of a tradition of kingship that Firdausi portrays as stretching back, unbroken, to the dawn of time.

Though little is known concerning the figure of Firdausi (died c. 1020) or the reasons for the composition of the *Shahnama*, the epic poem has traditionally been interpreted as a reassertion of Iranian identity almost four centuries after the Arab conquest of the Sasanian empire. If Firdausi had intended the *Shahnama* to revive something of Iran's kingly past, then he would have been satisfied with the fascination that the poem exerted on the subsequent rulers of Iran, who were from his time onwards almost exclusively of Turco-Mongol origin. The tradition of illustrating copies of Firdausi's poem was in fact established in the early fourteenth century under the aegis of the Mongol Ilkhanid dynasty, who chose the *Shahnama* as the subject for perhaps the most spectacular illustrated manuscript of the period, the Great Mongol *Shahnama*, or so-called Demotte *Shahnama*.[1]

The preference shown towards Persian and artistic literary traditions by all the Turco-Mongol dynasties east of Egypt meant that by the sixteenth century CE the status of Persian as one of the principal imperial and literary languages was assured in the realms

Isfandiyar kills Bidarafsh, no. 25, f. 390v (detail)
In the reign of King Gushtasp, the King's brother Zarir was killed in battle by the Turanian hero Bidarafsh. Here Isfandiyar, the son of Gushtasp, avenges the death of Zarir by slaying Bidarafsh on the battlefield. The Turanian army, thrown into confusion as a result, fled. Following the battle, the magnanimous Isfandiyar prevented the slaughter of the Turanian foe, moved by their cries for mercy.

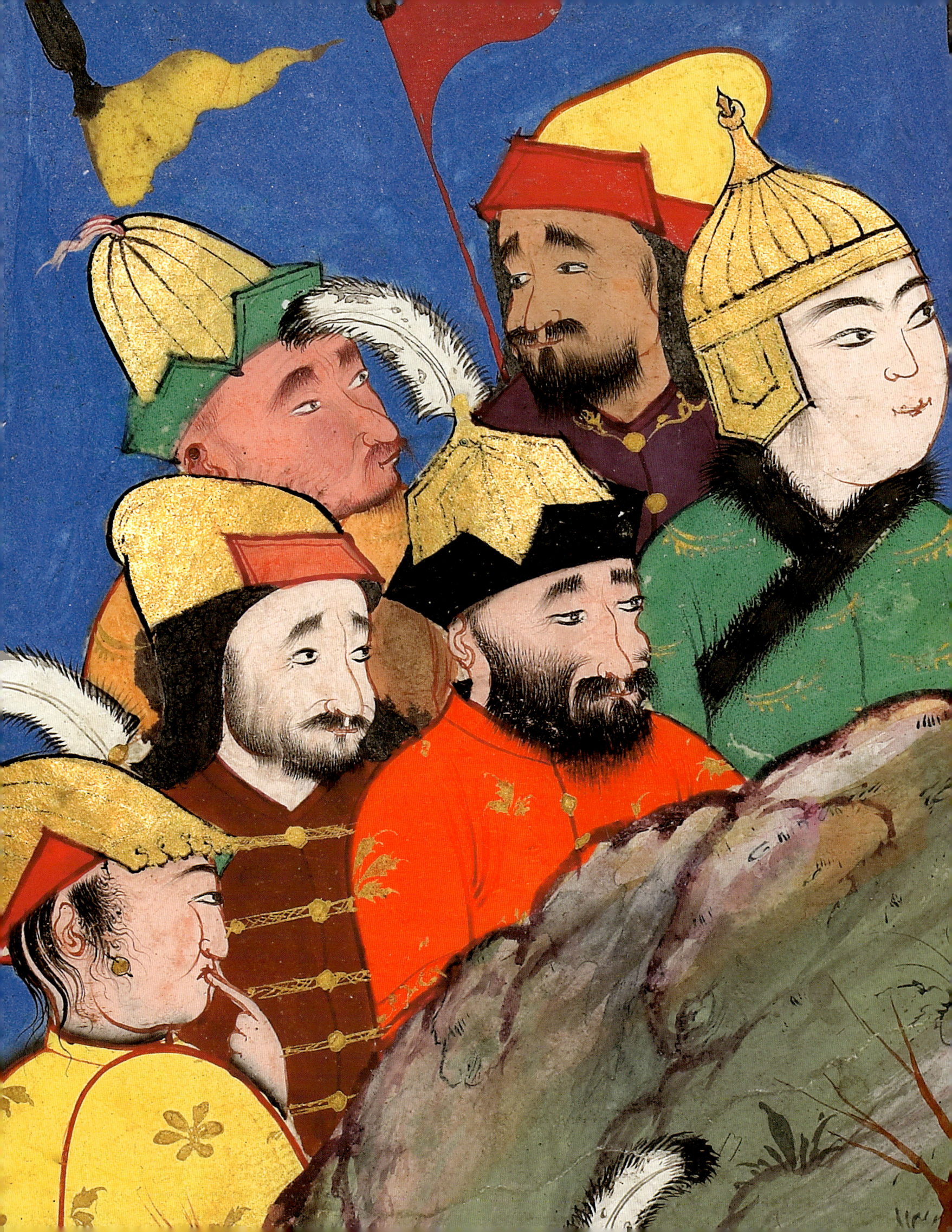

of the Ottoman, Safavid and Mughal Empires. Though political and ideological rivals, all three empires were of Turkic origin and belonged to the same Persianate cultural universe. In this shared ethos Iranian notions of royal legitimacy continued to figure large, and the tradition of commissioning illustrated versions of Firdausi's epic was perpetuated in all three empires.

The present manuscript, the Eckstein *Shahnama*, is a witness both to the shared cultural world that these empires inhabited and the political and ideological rivalries that divided them. It is a member of a well-known and controversial group of late sixteenth- and early seventeenth-century copies of Firdausi's *Shahnama*, often referred to as the 'truncated *Shahnamas*' since they present a reduced version of Firdausi's text. Recent research has pointed to the Ottoman Empire as the origin of these manuscripts,[2] and, as we shall see, analysis of the Eckstein *Shahnama* supports this thesis. In addition to various textual idiosyncrasies pointing to an origin outside the Iranian heartlands, the manuscript seems to present a peculiarly Ottoman version of Iranian history that must have had particular resonance in the context of the Ottoman-Safavid war. In 1584, the year in which the text of the Eckstein *Shahnama* was copied, the Ottoman Empire was attempting to expand its eastern frontier at the expense of its political and ideological enemy, the Safavid Empire. Their bitter conflict was to last until 1590, at which point the young Safavid ruler Shah 'Abbas, anxious to bring an end to twelve years of draining warfare, ceded to Sultan Murad III considerable territories in the Caucasus and Caspian. Though Firdausi's epic at first sight might seem an unlikely vehicle for the expression of anti-Safavid sentiment, the analysis below suggests that the Eckstein *Shahnama* may have been informed by an ideology that implied the Ottomans' right to rule the Iranian heartlands then in the possession of their Safavid rivals.

If the late sixteenth century was a period of intense political and ideological confrontation between these two great Islamic empires, it was also one of cultural exchange during which Iranian artistic traditions exerted a strong influence in the Ottoman Empire, notably in the arts of the book. The Eckstein *Shahnama* is particularly well placed to be an illustration of this almost paradoxical situation: while partaking in an Ottoman view of Iranian history, the Eckstein *Shahnama* is nonetheless somehow the most 'Iranian' of the truncated *Shahnama* series, a quality that, as we shall see, may have been quite deliberate in the context of its ideological outlook. The Eckstein *Shahnama* stands out from the core group of truncated *Shahnamas* on account of the presence in it of sixteen paintings in a late sixteenth-century Qazvin court style that has been traditionally associated with the work of the Safavid court artist 'Ali Asghar. Analysis of the styles and iconography of these and other paintings in the Eckstein *Shahnama* reveal quite precisely the ways in which Iranian styles of painting reached the Ottoman Empire, in what contexts they were deemed particularly appropriate, and how they were subsequently transformed.

The following essay is a study of the manuscript, beginning with a physical and textual description and moving on to an examination of the painting styles. The second half of the study discusses the ideological implications of the Eckstein *Shahnama* and situates the paintings in the context of the transference of Iranian styles in a process that linked prophecy, Iranian history and dynastic legitimacy.

Detail from *The first combat: Fariburz kills Gulbad*, no. 22, f. 322v

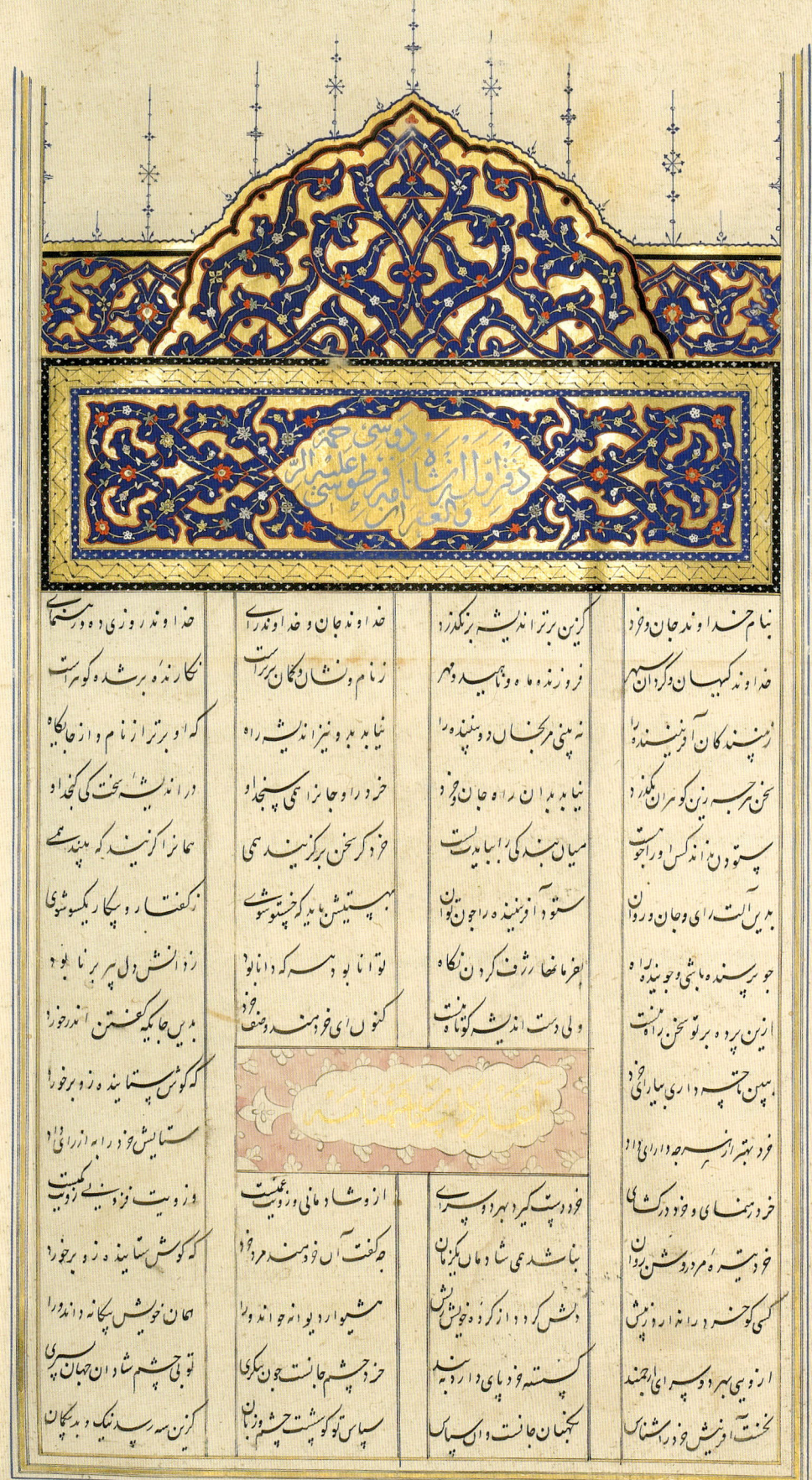

Illuminated chapter heading, f. 8v

The Manuscript

Description of the Manuscript

The Eckstein *Shahnama* consists of 585 numbered folios, each measuring 46 x 33.5 cm, and an additional blank folio at the beginning of the manuscript. The manuscript is in pristine condition, with only a few water stains. The paper is thick, glossy (burnished), and a very pale cream colour, and is one of the many indications of an Ottoman provenance for the Eckstein *Shahnama*. Though there was no home-based paper industry in the Ottoman Empire, the Ottomans preferred an almost white paper with small brown flecks, which was probably manufactured for them according to specification from paper-making centres in Iran and Syria. The Safavids, on the other hand, seem to have preferred a brown paper of a more consistent texture for their own manuscripts.[3]

The text block, including the frame, measures 31 x 19.25 cm and consists of 21 lines of *nastaliq* script in a neat sixteenth-century hand. The text is divided into four columns, divided by double intercolumnar rules in gold. The whole text block is ruled with blue and gold margins. The *'unvans* (chapter headings) and sub-chapter headings are written in a gold *thulth* script.

The Eckstein *Shahnama* contains thirty-two illustrations in a variety of styles that appear to have been executed by several artists. At least six paintings were removed from the manuscript, probably in the early twentieth century. Catchwords are written in the same hand as the main body of the text. One of these would seem to indicate that a seventh folio is missing (ff. 558–59), but the use of a textual variant raises the possibility that in fact the wrong catchword has been supplied, and, given that all six of the removed illustrations appeared for sale as a group in 1976,[4] this appears to be the more likely explanation. At some point after the removal of these pages the folios were numbered, though clearly incorrectly, as one folio (between ff. 258 and 259) has been missed.

Colophons and Later Provenance

On the final folio there is a colophon bearing the date 29 Dhu'l-Hijja 991 (12 January 1584), though unfortunately the names of the scribe and the scribe's father have been erased. On f. 1r there is an inscription stating that the manuscript belonged to 'Ali Naqi Mirza Rukn al-Dawla, grandson of Muhammad Shah and governor of Khurasan and Kerman at the beginning of the twentieth century.[5] We know that the manuscript was in an Ottoman collection prior to this, however: opposite each miniature small sheets of European cream paper have been inserted, some of which bear Ottoman

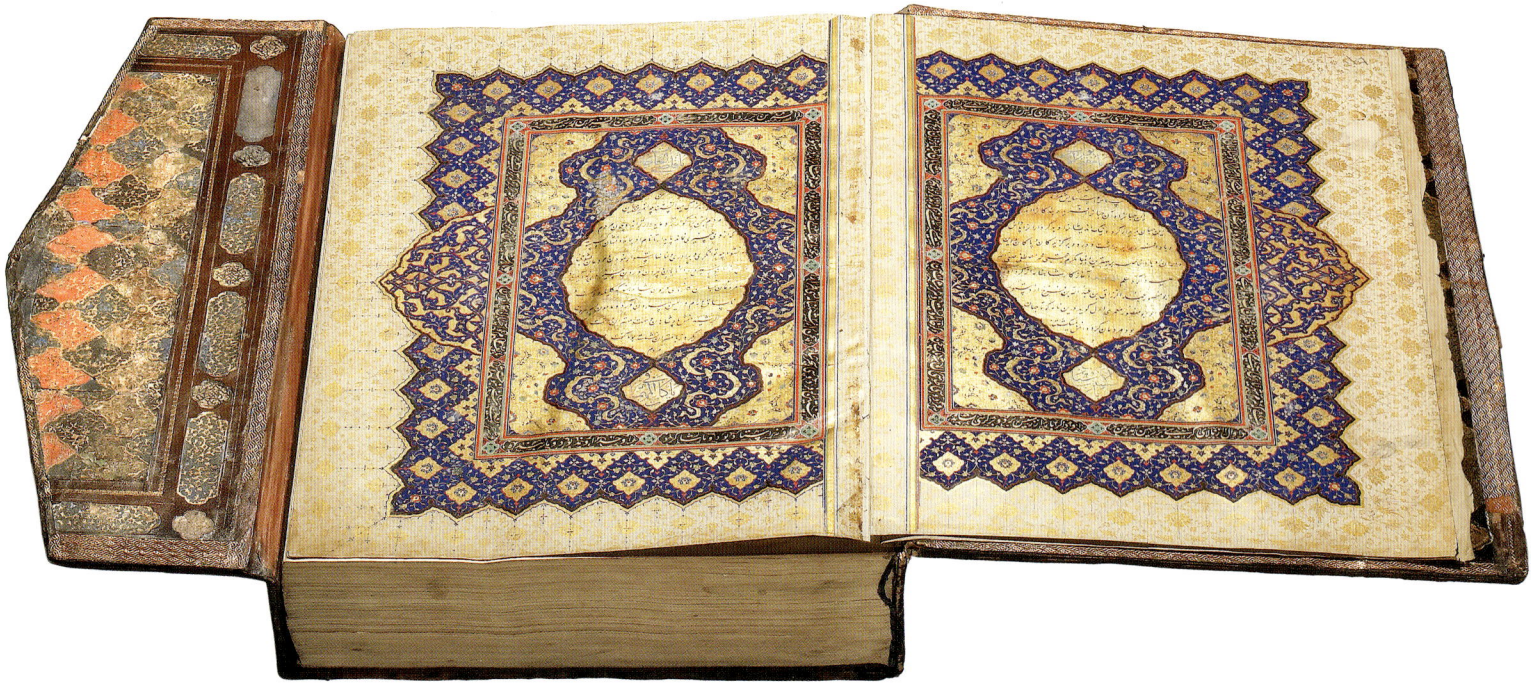

The Eckstein *Shahnama*

Turkish descriptions of the relevant miniature in a seventeenth-century hand.

A note in French on f. 1r is written in a hand identifiable as that of Georges Demotte, suggesting that the manuscript passed into the possession of the French dealer at some point in the early twentieth century.[6] In 1935 the manuscript was acquired by the collector Sir Bernard Eckstein, most of whose oriental collection was bequeathed to the British Museum in 1948.[7] The Eckstein *Shahnama*, however, was put into sale at Sotheby's a year later, at which point it was acquired by the Hagop Kevorkian Collection.[8]

The Binding

Though probably contemporary with the manuscript, the binding is not the original one. This is apparent on the recto side of the opening blank folio, which contains the offset of the inside cover of a binding that does not correspond to that of the present one. In addition, part of the bird alighting in the tree in the top margin on f. 119v has been cut off at the top of the page, which would indicate that the manuscript has been trimmed.

The binding that now contains the Eckstein *Shahnama* is typical of sixteenth-century Safavid manuscripts. The outer covers are of painted, stamped, tooled and gilded leather. The pattern is identical on the front and back covers and consists of a central lobed ogival medallion with a palmette above and below each end, in addition to four lobed corner-pieces and four half-palmettes, two on each long side of the central panel. The border consists of two bands, the outer thicker than the inner, of cartouches alternating with quatrefoils. The central medallion, corner pieces, palmettes and outer border are all filled with a combination of lotus blossom and *rumi* scrolls, while the area surrounding the medallion and the inner band of cartouches have lotus-blossom scrolls and cloud bands. The inside covers consist of lobed, interlocking blue, orange and turquoise shapes formed by placing gold floral filigree over coloured paper. These are surrounded by a border of alternating cartouches and quatrefoils, contained within a border of a gold wave pattern.

The Organization of the Manuscript

I The truncated *Shahnamas*

The Eckstein *Shahnama* belongs to the group of 'truncated' *Shahnamas*, so called on account of the abbreviated version of Firdausi's epic they relate. The truncated *Shahnamas* either end with the reign of Alexander, as is the case in the Eckstein *Shahnama*, or with the reign of Queen Humay, daughter and wife of Bahman, omitting the 'historical' sections of the *Shahnama* that cover the reigns of the Parthian and Sasanian kings up to the Arab conquests. In addition, the truncated *Shahnamas* include one or more of four of the post-*Shahnama* epics, the *Samnama*, the *Barzunama*, the *Garshaspnama* and the *Bahmannama*. These epics, in a style close to the 'popular' epics of Iran and Anatolia, elaborate on the deeds and adventures of various kings and heroes mentioned in the *Shahnama*, among whom the family of the hero Rustam is particularly prominent.

The truncated *Shahnamas* range in date from around 1573 to the first quarter of the seventeenth century. A seminal study has identified a group of nine truncated *Shahnamas*, including the Eckstein *Shahnama*, dating from the 1570s and 1580s, the paintings of which are clearly related to the output of the ateliers responsible for a series of *Qisas al-Anbiya'* (Stories of the Prophets) manuscripts from the same period. As the *Qisas* manuscripts had already been attributed to the Ottoman Empire, this attribution was extended to the truncated *Shahnama* group. In addition to the highly unusual version of Firdausi's text, other distinctive features such as additional prefaces extolling the virtues of Firdausi and the *Shahnama*, and double-page miniatures, supported the case for a non-Iranian attribution.[9] The Eckstein *Shahnama*, as we shall see, also directly influenced truncated *Shahnama* manuscripts from the early seventeenth century. The Eckstein *Shahnama*'s role as a 'bridge' between the group of nine *Shahnamas* of the 1570s and 1580s and the truncated *Shahnamas* of the seventeenth century can be seen as an argument for the Ottoman origin of the latter group of manuscripts too.

II The preface

Unusual among *Shahnamas* from the sixteenth century onwards, but typical of the truncated *Shahnama* series, is the preface to the Eckstein *Shahnama*. This belongs to the type identified by Mirza Muhammad Qazvini as the 'old' preface, though like those of some of the other truncated *Shahnamas* it contains additional sections.[10] The information contained in these is found in the major sources for Firdausi's

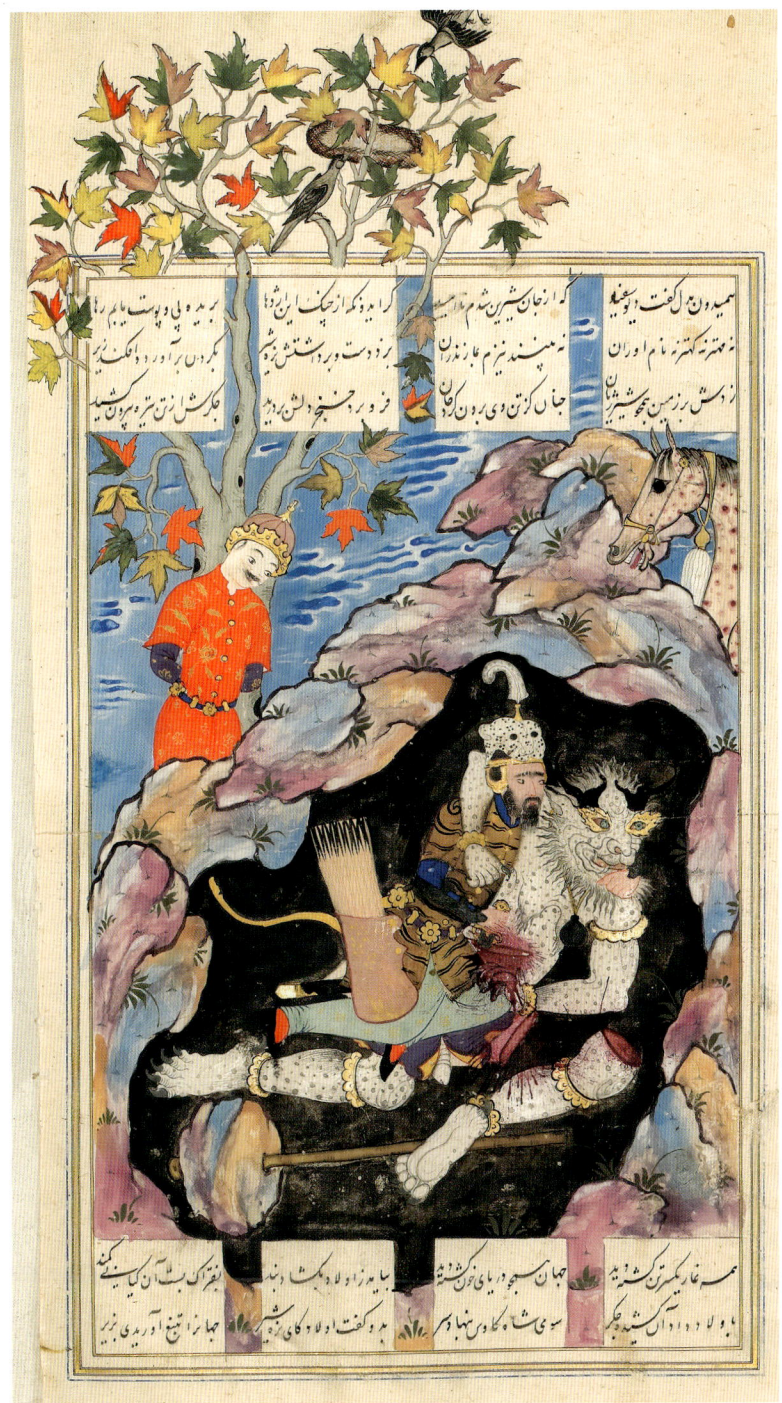

Rustam's seventh labour: he kills the White Div, no. 11, f. 119v

One of the kings of Iran, Kay Ka'us, had been captured by a formidable demon, the White Div, and tied to a tree next to his lair in the mountains of Mazandaran. Rustam, presented with the choice of following an easy but slow route or one fraught with danger that could be covered in seven days, immediately chose the latter. The last obstacle faced by the hero was a hand-to-hand struggle with the demon himself. Having overcome the demon, Rustam cut out his liver and anointed the eyes of the King with the blood from it.

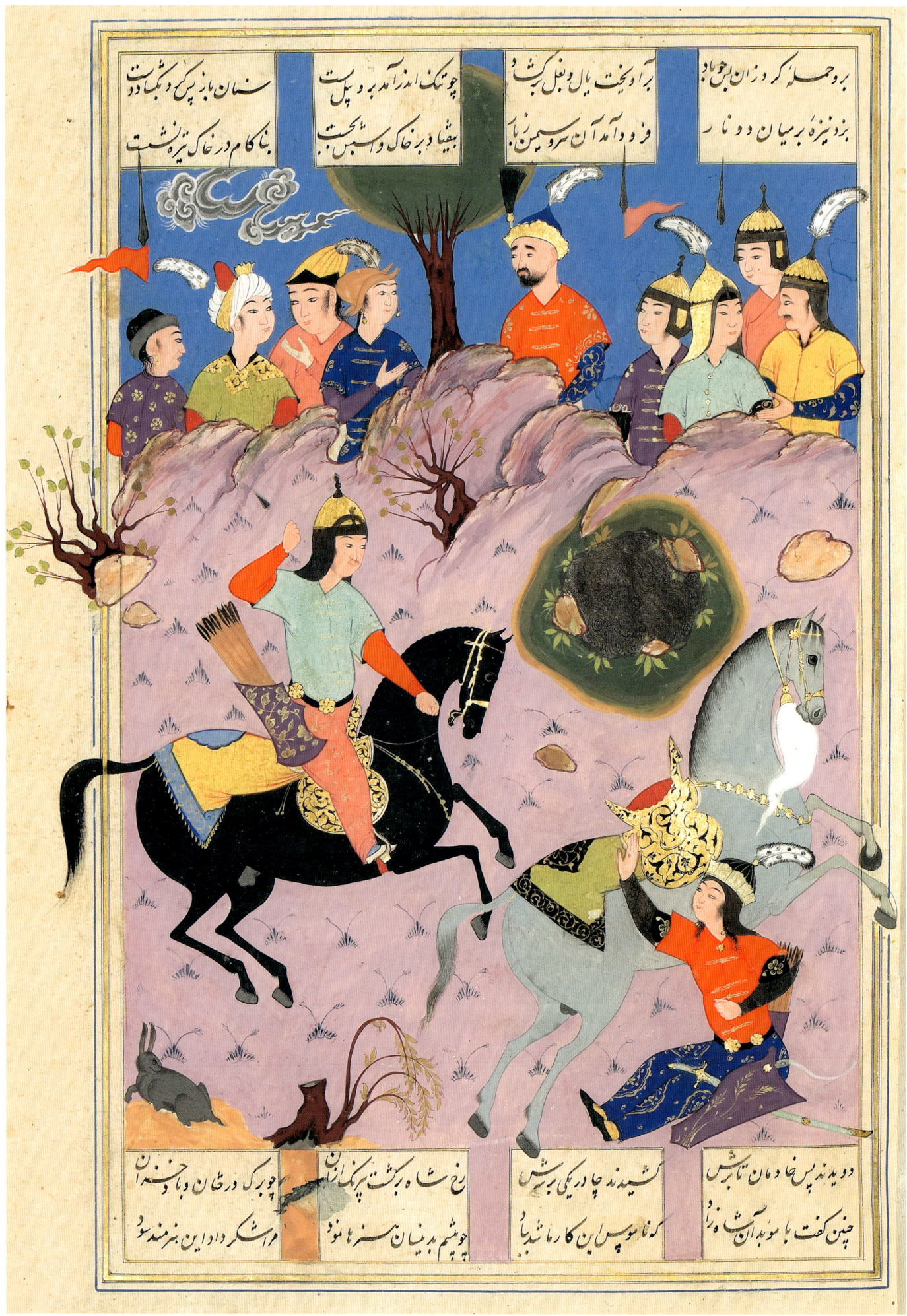

Bahman fights Humay, no. 28, f. 453r (detail)

The painting depicts a scene from the *Bahmannama*, one of the post-*Shahnama* epics most frequently interpolated into Firdausi's text. In the *Bahmannama*, Bahman, the son of Isfandiyar, is deposed by the machinations of his adulterous first wife, the daughter of the King of Kashmir. Bahman is forced to flee to Egypt, where he encounters an army led by Humay, the daughter of the King of Egypt, who he later marries.

life such as the Baysunghur preface, Nizami 'Arudi's *Chahar Maqala* and Dawlatshah's *Tadhkirat al-Shu'ara'*, though some major variations from the versions presented in these sources suggest that the prefaces to the truncated *Shahnamas* form part of a tradition that evolved separately from the mainstream Iranian tradition.

The first section of the preface to the Eckstein *Shahnama* is very close to the edition of the 'old' preface edited by Qazvini and relates the story of the translation of the *Kalila wa Dimna* from Pahlavi to Arabic on the orders of Harun al-Rashid, and from Arabic to Persian on the orders of the Samanid amir Nasr ibn Ahmad. Thereafter, in accordance with the version presented in the 'old' preface, it gives an account of the beginning of the compilation of a prose account of the reigns and deeds of the kings of Iran, carried out under the auspices of Abu Mansur al-Ma'mari, the minister of the governor of Tus, Amir Mansur 'Abd al-Razzaq. According to the preface, it was this work that was given to the poet Daqiqi to versify, a task left to Firdausi after the assassination of the former by a Turkish slave boy with whom he was besotted.

The preface then goes on to give a defence of the *Shahnama* and the utility of such books as reliable histories and as didactic works on kingship. A justification for relying on ancient Persian wisdom is provided by an analogy with the Prophet Muhammad's sanction of the use of the knowledge of the Banu Isra'il, the Jews. This is followed by an account of the Avestan division of the world that has 'Iranzamin', Greater Iran, as its centre. A curious detail, but one consistent with other versions of the 'old' preface, is the designation of the Nile as Iranzamin's western border, and not the Euphrates, which was the standard in most medieval Persian accounts.

There follows an attempt to coordinate the version of events and the beginning of the world in the *Shahnama* with Islamic/Judaeo-Christian history, and a long section detailing the genealogies of both Mansur al-Ma'mari and Mansur 'Abd al-Razzaq, both of which lead back to pre-Islamic Iranian heroes.

At this point, where Qazvini's version of the 'old' preface ends, the Eckstein *Shahnama* continues with the story of Daqiqi's demise at the hands of his slave boy and Firdausi's assumption of the task of completing the *Shahnama* at the request of Sultan Mahmud of Ghazna. The account contains some elements of the version of events found in 'Arudi's *Chahar Maqala*, though with some substantial differences. Whereas in 'Arudi's version it is Firdausi who presents his work to Sultan Mahmud of Ghazna, the Eckstein *Shahnama* preface remains faithful to the 'old' preface in attributing the conception of the project to Mahmud. The Eckstein *Shahnama* preface

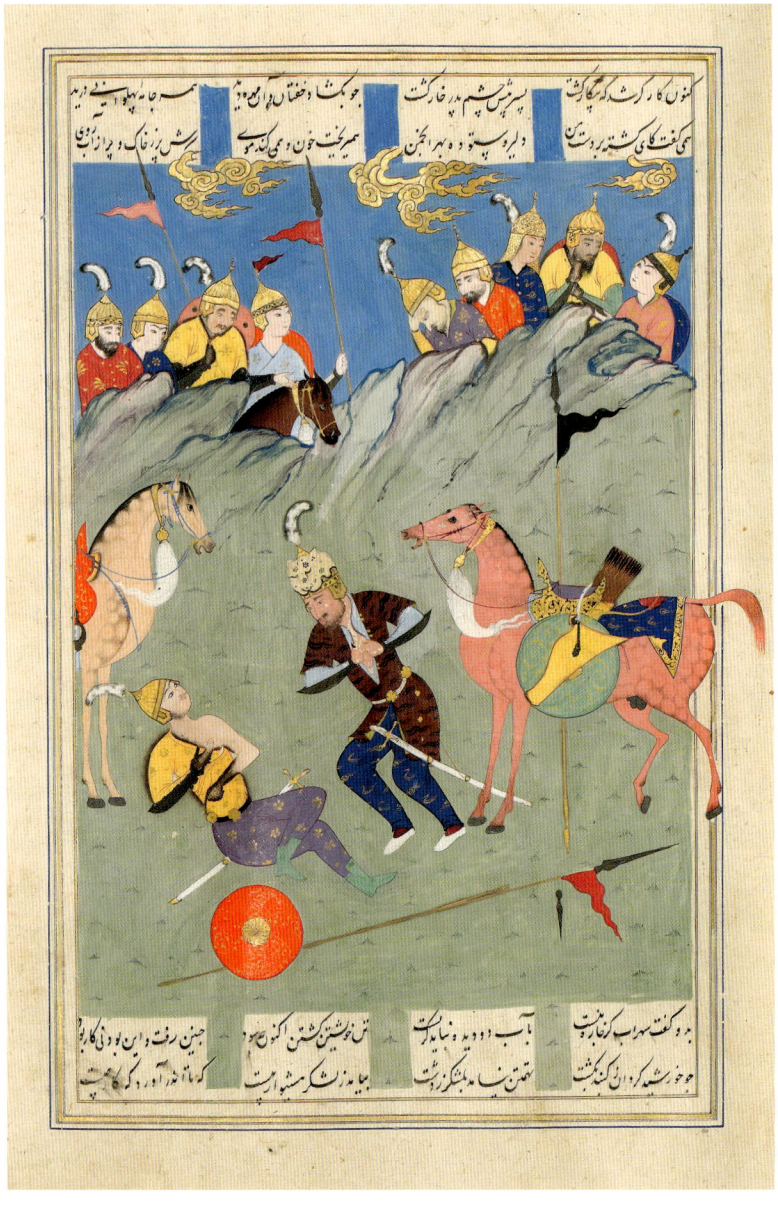

ABOVE *Rustam discovers Suhrab's identity*, no. 13, f. 146r

A tragic episode in the *Shahnama* is Rustam's unwitting slaughter of his own son, Suhrab. Rustam had extracted a promise from a local princess with whom he had had an affair that she should alert him should she bear him a child. The princess kept the boy's birth a secret from his father, however. The wily king of Turan, Afrasiyab, realising the danger that a father-son alliance might pose, managed to pit Rustam and Suhrab against each other in battle, concealing the identity of each from the other. Only after Rustam had stabbed Suhrab did he see the jewel he had entrusted to the boy's mother.

RIGHT *Isfandiyar kills Arjasp to rescue his sisters*, no. 26, f. 408r

Arjasp, the king of Turan, had captured Isfandiyar's sisters, the daughters of King Gushtasp of Iran. Isfandiyar and his companions gained access to the Turanian king's fortress disguised as merchants. Once inside, they hosted a party, waiting to catch the carousing Turanians off-guard. Isfandiyar himself decapitates Arjasp, later flinging his head over the ramparts of the fortress.

follows 'Arudi's account in reporting Mahmud's dissatisfaction with the work, but relates a different version of Firdausi's visit to the bathhouse. In 'Arudi's version of events Firdausi distributes the meagre reward given him by Sultan Mahmud to a bath attendant and a beer seller; the preface to the Eckstein *Shahnama*, however, has Firdausi distribute the 60,000 gold dinars which the repentant Sultan sends him. The 60,000 dinars appear in Arudi's account, but reach the poet just as his funeral procession is leaving the city.

The Eckstein *Shahnama*, then, presents an alternative version of events, though one close to the story related in the Baysunghur preface. As in that preface, Firdausi is portrayed as the son of a landlord who sets out for the court of the Sultan to seek redress against the oppression of a local tax-collector. Once in Ghazna he chances upon the company of the three famous poets and out-manoeuvres them in a rhyming competition in which they try to trick him. From this point onwards, however, the version presented in the Eckstein *Shahnama* differs. In the Baysunghuri preface the poets of Ghazna, headed by 'Unsuri, realising the threat Firdausi's talent poses, conspire to prevent him from reaching the Sultan. With the assistance of his friend, Mahak, however, he is able to bring his work to the attention of the Sultan. Impressed by Firdausi's poetry, the Sultan presents the court with a challenge: whosoever can better Firdausi's verses will be rewarded with the task of completing the *Shahnama*. At this point, 'Unsuri, realizing the futility of any opposition, publicly acknowledges Firdausi's superiority and recommends him for the task. In the Eckstein *Shahnama*'s simpler, perhaps more introductory version, 'Unsuri, upon being overwhelmed by Firdausi's talent, brings him to the court of Mahmud. Here, Mahmud, bowled over by a panegyric addressed to him, commissions Firdausi to complete the *Shahnama*.

The history of the various versions of the prefaces to the *Shahnama* is far from clear, and the textual genealogy of the prefaces used in the Eckstein *Shahnama* calls for further investigation. One can speculate, however, that the decision to use the more rudimentary 'old' preface in most of the truncated *Shahnamas* may have been due to the intended audience's unfamiliarity with the work. Presumably, by the late sixteenth century CE, to an Iranian reader or audience much of the information it contains would have seemed superfluous, because the work was so well known. The opening lines of the preface are contained in the medallions on each page of the opening frontispiece. This in itself presents nothing unusual, though the amount of text included in these is much larger than is normally the case; but this detail, in addition to the poetry in praise of Firdausi

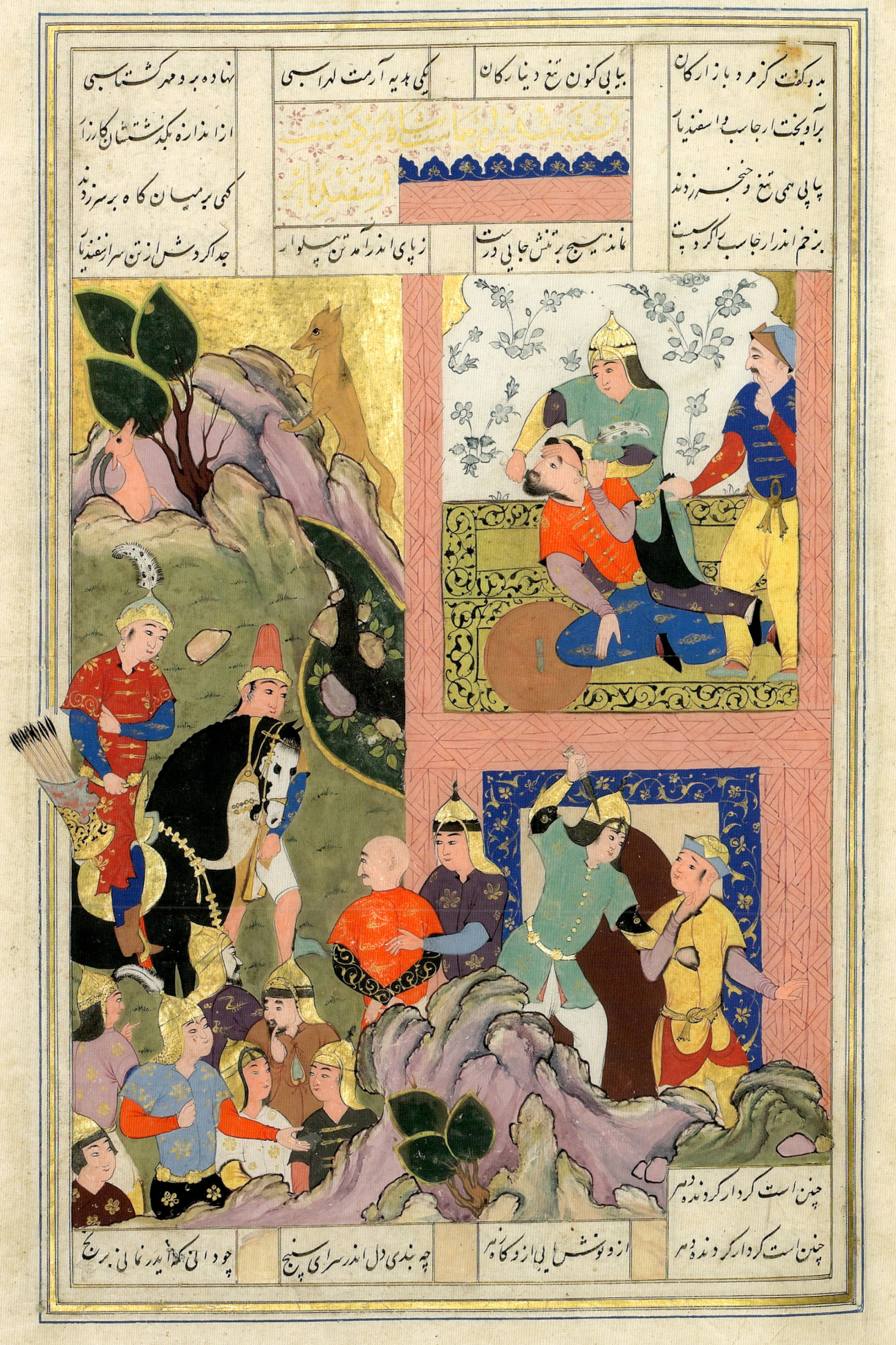

contained in the bands surrounding the central illuminated panel, would also suggest that the reader was not completely familiar with Firdausi's work and needed some sort of justification for reading it. Again, this situation would be unthinkable in a late sixteenth-century Iranian context.[11]

In addition, textual peculiarities in the Eckstein *Shahnama* would suggest that even the copyist was not completely familiar with Firdausi's *Shahnama* or the well-established legend that surrounded it. While textual variants are to be expected in a genre that was so intimately bound up with oral tradition, some variations are clearly scribal errors. The most obvious of these is the misspelling of Ibn Muqaffa', the translator of the *Kalila wa Dimna* from Pahlavi to Arabic, as 'Ibn Muqanna'' or 'Ibn Muqni'', depending on one's reading of the vocalization. Moreover, according to the preface Ibn Muqaffa' did not translate the work from Pahlavi to Arabic, but the other way round (f. 2v)! Other misspellings of proper names include 'Ruzbih' for 'Barzuy', the physician and translator of the *Kalila wa Dimna* from Sanskrit to Pahlavi, 'Hajar Isfahani' for 'Hamza Isfahani', and 'Sisan' for 'Sistan' (f. 2v). Another error is found on f. 3r, where the scribe has mistakenly used the word *savad*, 'literacy', instead of *sud*, 'benefit'. On f. 2v Yazdagird, the last of the Sasanian kings, is erroneously called 'the last of the kings of Kayan' – another indication that the scribe was not familiar with Firdausi's text or Iranian history. This is suggested again by the repetition of certain items in a list on f. 3r of the various actions and moods that can be found in the *Shahnama*, including *parhiz*, 'caution', and *andar shudan* as part of the phrase *andar shudan va birun shudan*, 'entering and exiting'. This, and such mistakes as the repetition of the conjunction *va*, 'and', on f. 4r, strike one as the errors of someone not fully in command of the meaning or grammar of the text he was copying.

III **The division of the manuscript**
The most unusual aspect of the Eckstein *Shahnama* is the division of the text into eleven *daftars,* or chapters, a division that as far as we know is without precedent. The chapters vary in length from 24 folios (Chapter 11) to 130 folios (Chapter 10). Each chapter is marked with an elaborately illuminated heading (*'unvan*), and is divided into several sub-chapters indicated by smaller headings of which the illumination appears unfinished. Though plain headings with the interstices filled in with pink or yellow cross-hatching are not unknown, the lavish illumination of the frontispiece and *'unvans* in the Eckstein *Shahnama* suggest that the sub-chapter headings were intended to be similarly ornate. The incomplete state of the

Detail from *Rustam pulls the Khaqan of Chin from his elephant*, no. 17, f. 240v

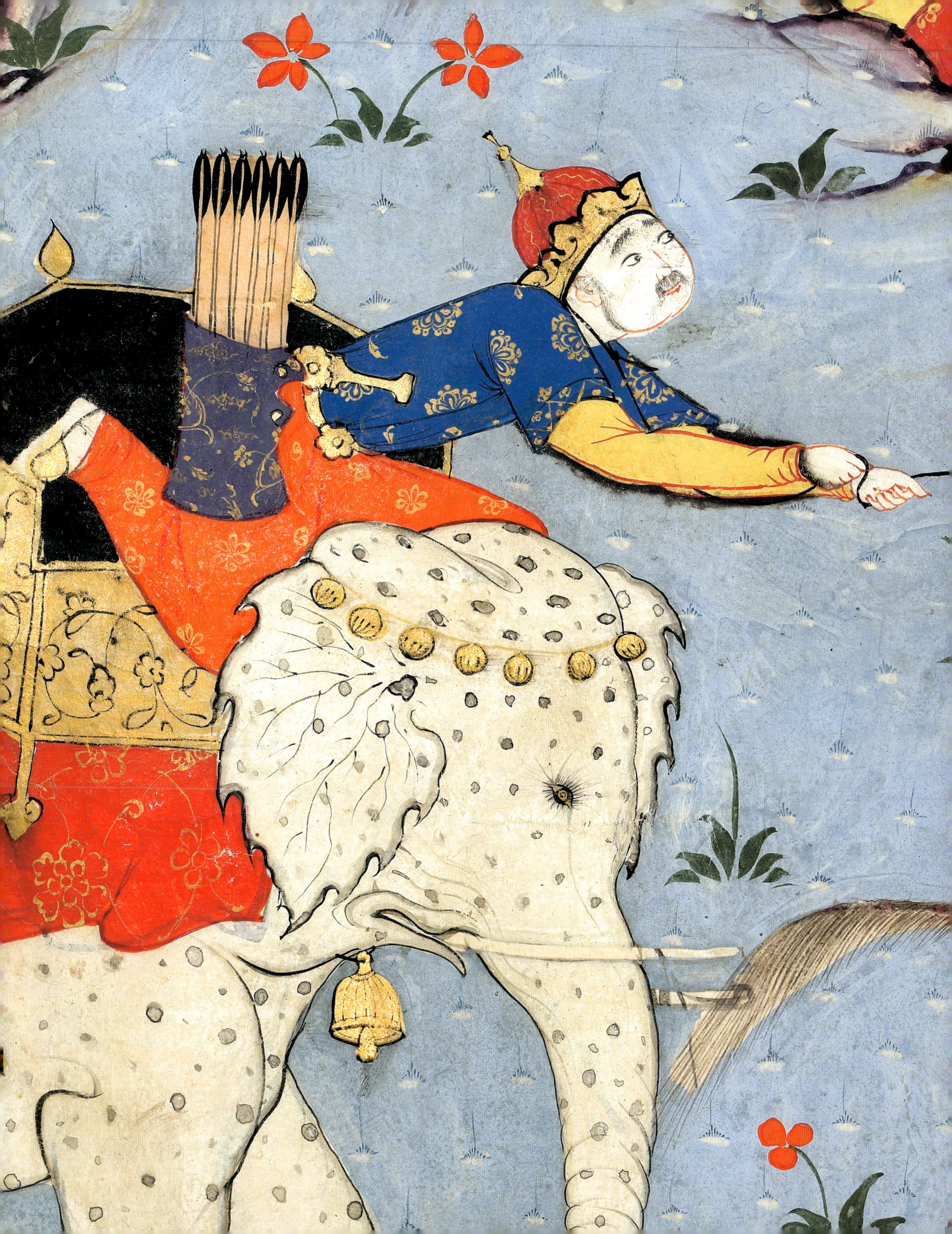

frontispiece, too (see discussion on page 24), would corroborate this hypothesis.

The chapter headings and the headings for the sub-sections are in a very fine gold *thulth*, though where the scribe was short for space he added the final words in a small *nastaliq*. The eleven chapters are entitled as follows:

1 'The first chapter of the *Shahnama* of Firdausi, may God bless and forgive him' (f. 8v) [30 ff.]
2 'The second chapter from the tale of the *Shahnama* concerning Sam and one of his love affairs' (f. 38v) [37 ff.]
3 'The third chapter concerning the abandonment of the mother of Zal, son of Sam-i Nariman' (f. 75v) [57 ff.]
4 'The fourth chapter from the tale of the *Shahnama* concerning the story of Suhrab son of Rustam' (f. 132v) [27 ff.]
5 'The fifth chapter and the discovery [?] of Siyavush' (f. 149r) [103 ff.]
6 'The sixth chapter concerning the story of the *Bizhannama*' (f. 252v) [28 ff.]
7 'The seventh chapter concerning the story of Barzu, son of Suhrab' (f. 270v) [29 ff.]
8 'The eighth chapter concerning the story of the Eleven Champions' (f. 299v) [72 ff.]
9 'The ninth chapter concerning the story of Gushtasp son of Suhrab (f. 371v) [60 ff.]
10 'The tenth chapter concerning the story of Bahman son of Isfandiyar' (f. 431v) [130 ff.]
11 'The eleventh chapter concerning the story of the *Iskandarnama*' (f. 561v) [24 ff.]

IV **The headings**

Examination of the headings alone in the Eckstein *Shahnama* confirms that the scribe cannot have been a native speaker of Persian. Immediately striking is the use of variations in the orthography of the names of the heroes. Though some of these are standard, such as 'Siyavakhsh' for 'Siyavush' (*e.g.* f. 151r) and 'Sudava' for 'Sudaba' (*e.g.* f. 152v), the inconsistency in their application and the use of different spellings within pages of each other suggests that the scribe was either working from multiple copies of the work or transcribing multiple recitations. Likewise, the decision whether to use Persian or the more limited and archaic orthography that reflected Arabic spelling (such as *jim* for *che*) is applied inconsistently, so that on one page 'Chin', China, will be spelt with a *che*, and two pages

Kay Khusrau throws Shida to the ground, no. 23, f. 340r
Shida, the son of the Turanian King Afrasiyab, was renowned for his bravery. During a battle against the Iranian forces, the prince challenged the Iranian King Kay Khusrau to a wrestling match, only to be overcome and slain.

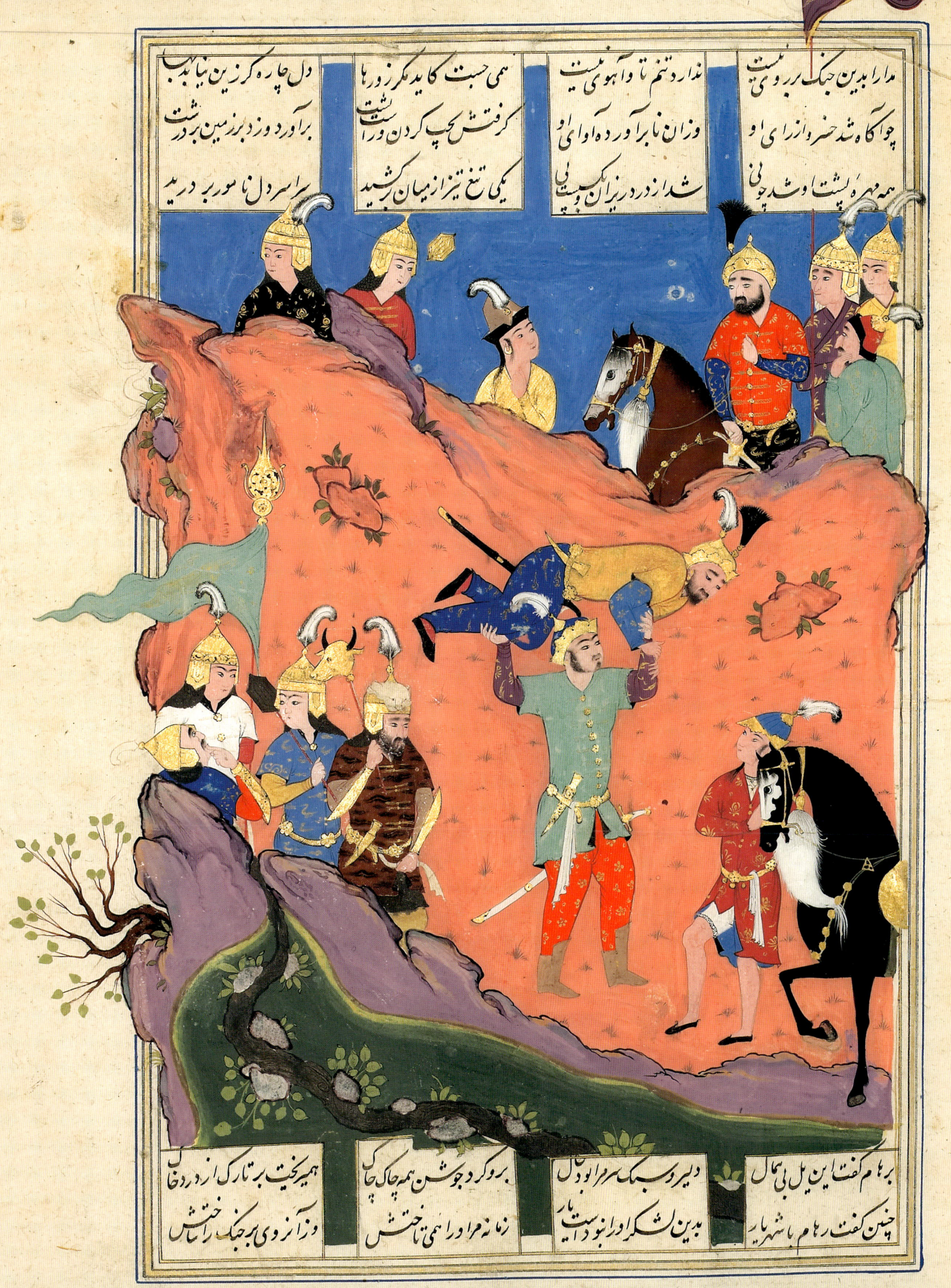

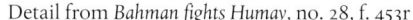

Detail from *Bahman fights Humay*, no. 28, f. 453r

later with a *jim* (*e.g.* ff. 65v and 67r). 'Paridukht' (f. 62r), the daughter of the King of China, alternates with 'Baridukht' (f. 55r), etc.

Other spellings are either extremely eccentric or simply orthographic errors. In addition to the variation on the name 'Sudaba' mentioned above, we also find it spelt 'Sudada' (f. 151r), which is without doubt a misspelling. 'Rudaba', the mother of the hero Rustam, is on f. 83r spelt 'Rudana'. 'Bizhan', though on occasion spelt correctly in the manuscript, is frequently misspelt 'Bizan' (*e.g.* f. 252v), and the word 'hazar', meaning a thousand, 'hizal' (f. 16r). On f. 37v 'Manuchihr' is misspelt 'Saruchihr', even though on the previous page the scribe had spelt it correctly. On f. 43r Sam's kingdom is correctly spelt as 'Khavarzamin' (land of the east), whereas on the previous folio it is misspelt 'Khadharzamin'. On f. 16r the scribe has spelt 'Mubidan' 'Mu'ayyidan', thus changing the meaning of the word from 'Zoroastrian priests' to 'helpers'! The same mistake is repeated on f. 92r. On f. 76r the letter *sin* in the word 'Simurgh' is written incorrectly with one of the 'teeth' missing, and the object marker 'ra' is misspelt 'za'. 'Zahhak', the evil king of Arabia, is misspelt 'Zuhhak' on f. 14v, and Mihrab, one of the champions of Turan, is spelt both 'Muhrab' (f. 103v) and 'Mahrab' (f. 90r).

The chapter and sub-chapter headings also contain examples of unidiomatic Persian. In several of the titles both the words *dastan* and *nama* are used, both of which mean 'story'. Though they could perhaps be translated respectively as 'tale' and 'book', nonetheless to a Persian speaker a title like 'Daftar-i yazdahum dar dastan-i [story of] *Iskandarnama* [the Tale of Alexander]' (f. 561v; illustrated on page 25), would have sounded uncomfortably tautological. Misspellings and scribal errors are of course frequently encountered in Persian manuscripts, interestingly most often in manuscripts where much attention has been paid to the illustrations and illumination.[12] The errors in the chapter and sub-chapter headings in the Eckstein *Shahnama*, however, which have been executed with great care and in a fine gold *thulth* script, are not so easily attributed to hasty copying. Unfamiliarity with Persian seems the more likely explanation and constitutes another indication of a provenance outside the Persian-speaking heartlands.

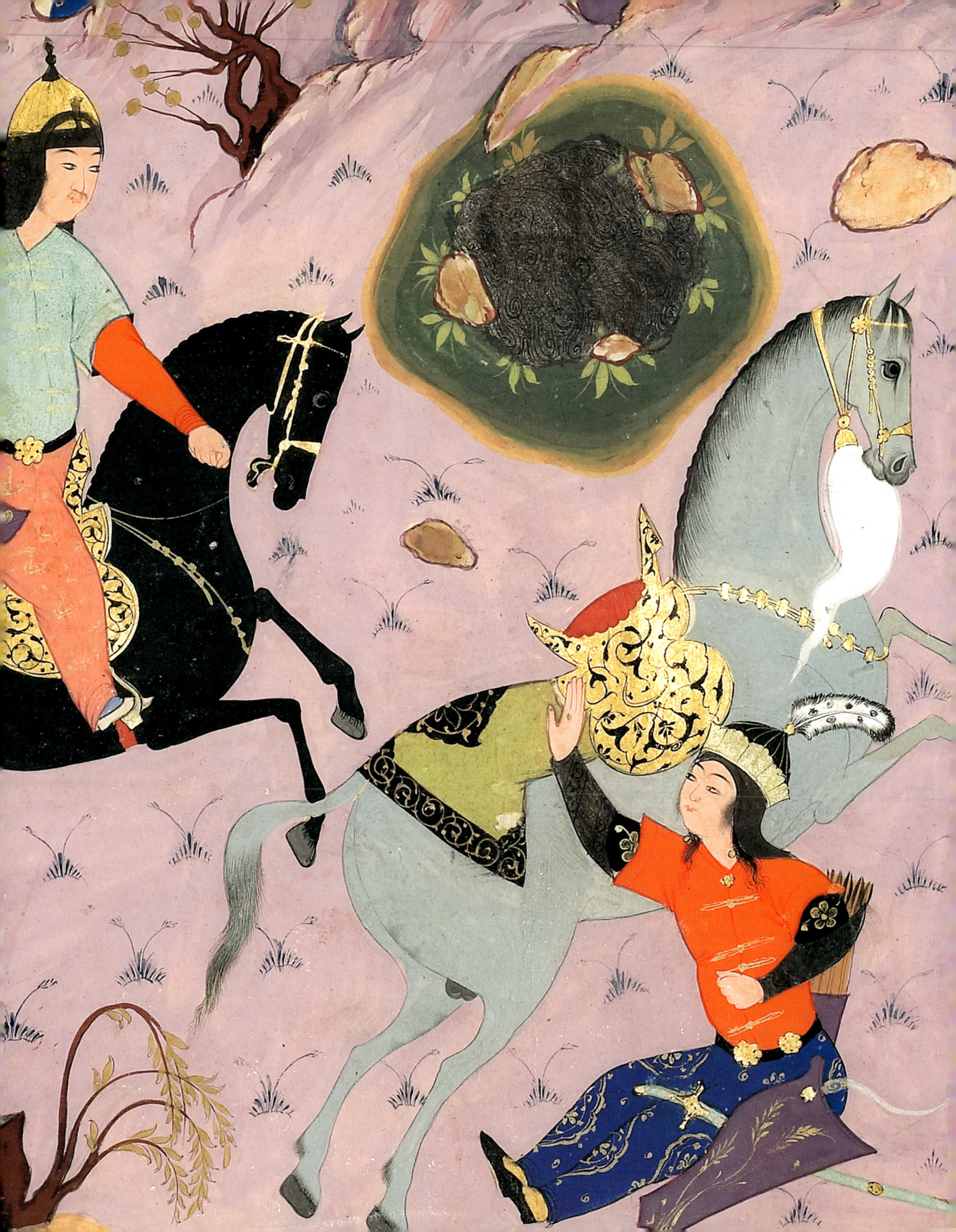

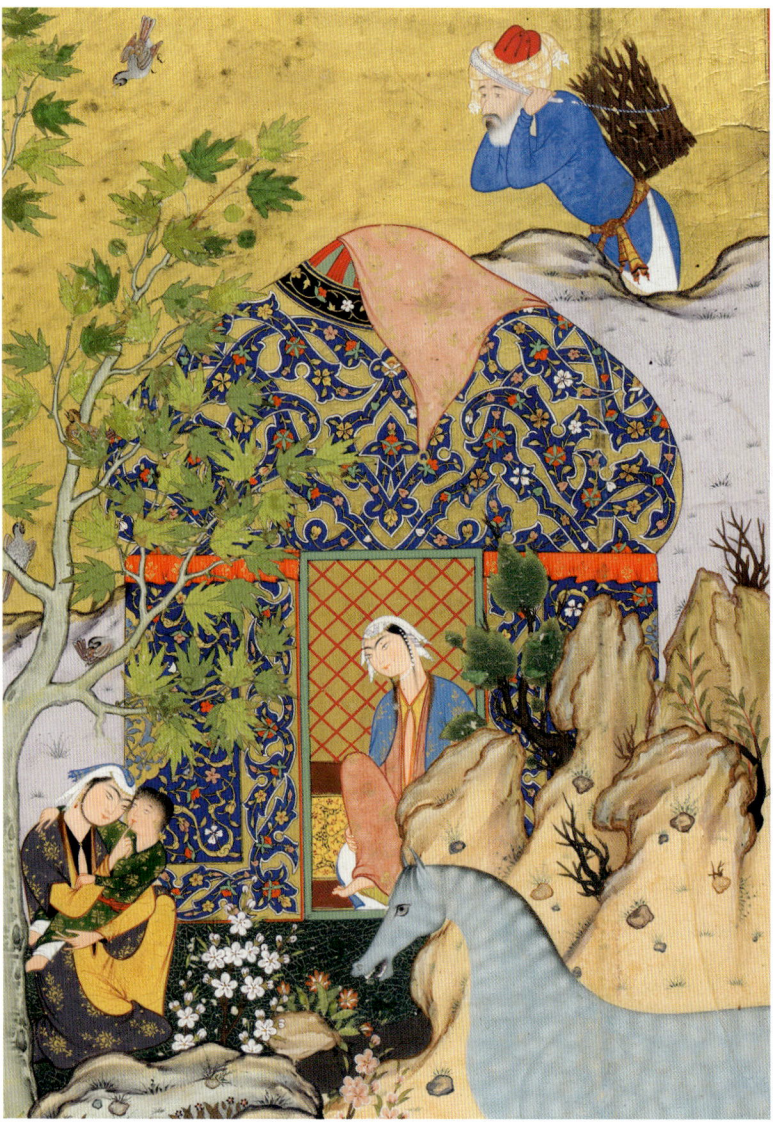

ABOVE Fig. 1 Detail from *Yusuf tends his flocks*, in *Haft Aurang*, Freer Gallery of Art, Washington, D.C., inv. 46.12, f. 110v

The blue and gold tendrils found on the tent in this painting were a staple of Iranian illumination from the second half of the sixteenth century. Though they were sometimes used to depict textiles, as here, their use in the Eckstein *Shahnama* in the central panel of some of the chapter headings (see opposite page) is highly unusual.

OPPOSITE ABOVE Illuminated chapter heading, f. 561v

OPPOSITE BELOW Illuminated chapter heading, f. 132v

The Illumination

The double-page frontispiece and the eleven chapter headings, illuminated in a style reminiscent of imperial Iranian illumination, constitute some of the highlights of the Eckstein *Shahnama*. The double-page frontispiece (see pages 26–27) is dominated by a large gold medallion in the centre of each page. The medallion contains the opening lines of the preface against a ground of deep blue, filled with an arabesque of gold-stemmed orange, turquoise and yellow flowers. Chinese-style cloud bands have been executed in two types of gold. The corner pieces are filled with floral and *rumi* scrolls; a burnished gold has been carefully applied in the execution of the stems and the *rumi* leaves in order to distinguish them from the liquid, coppery gold of the background. The inner border is ruled in orange and turquoise and contains long cartouches that enclose poems in praise of Firdausi, written in gold on a black ground. The cartouches are separated by turquoise quatrefoils, with the interstices filled in with red. The outer border contains bands of gold palmettes, each one with a lotus blossom in the centre, the lobed contours of which describe the lobed edge of the border. As in the central compartment, the blue ground is filled with floral scrolls and the edge has been delineated with thick black and gold rules. One of the most striking features of the frontispiece is the outsized *hasps* that project into the margin. These are filled with intertwined blue tendrils on a ground of burnished gold, and are of a type encountered frequently in high-quality illumination of the second half of the sixteenth century (see fig. 1). The surrounding area has been filled with scrolls of gold lotus blossoms. The illumination was apparently never finished, as the right-hand page is missing the thin blue line around the gold edge of the border and the projecting blue finials.

The eleven illuminated chapter headings are all based on a variation of the same model, mostly using features already encountered in the frontispiece: a rectangular panel contains a gold cartouche in which the chapter heading is invariably written in a blue *thulth*. The shape of the cartouche ranges from short and fat (f. 431v) to long and thin (f. 252r). The space within the central rectangle is filled with a variety of designs, nearly always on a blue ground. These range from a symmetrical design of four corner pieces with a quatrefoil on either side of the cartouche (f. 561v; see opposite page) to the blue tendrils set against the gold ground found in the projecting *hasps* of the frontispiece (ff. 8v, 132v; see page 10 and opposite page). The rectangular area is always bordered by a thick

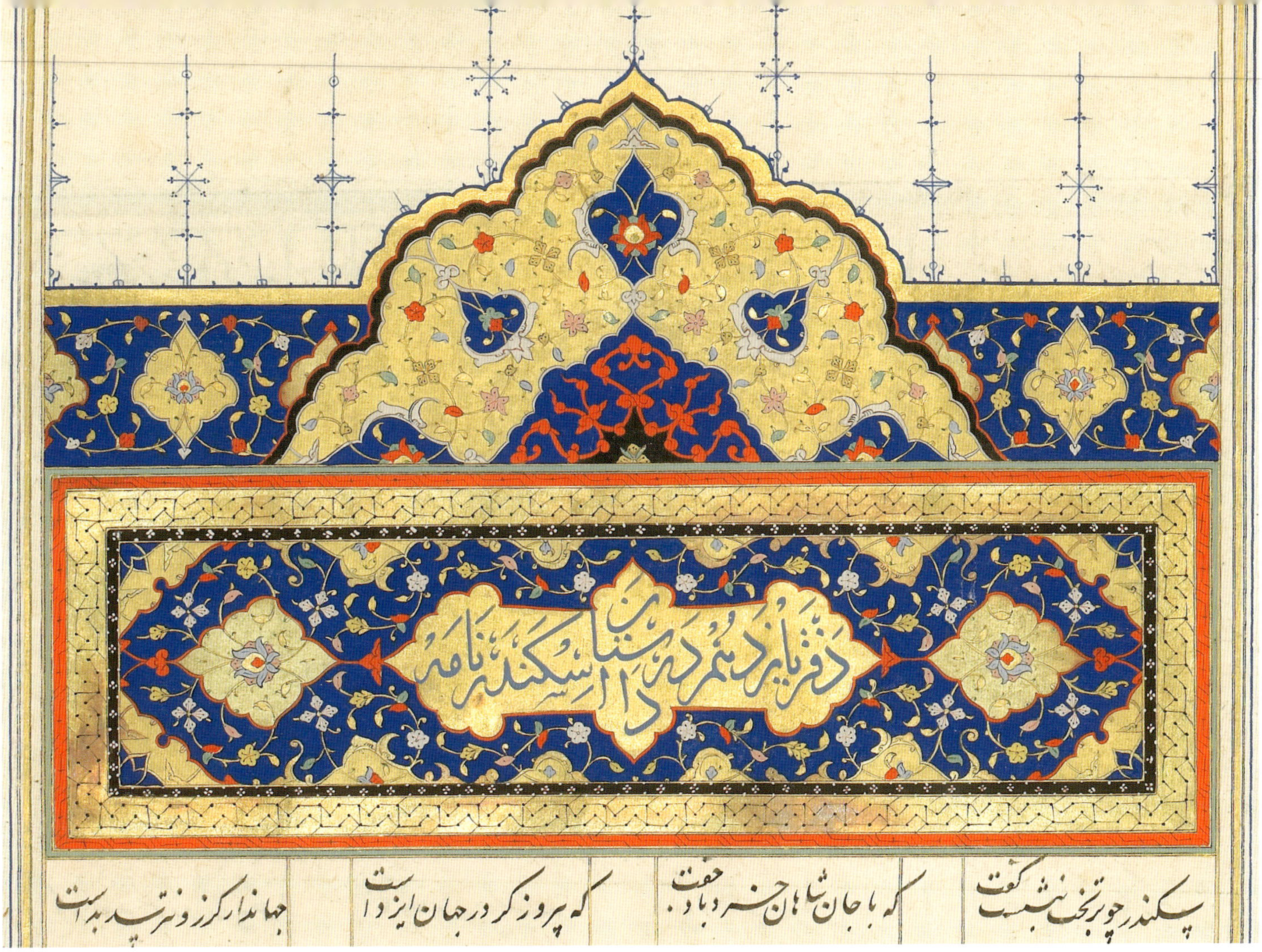

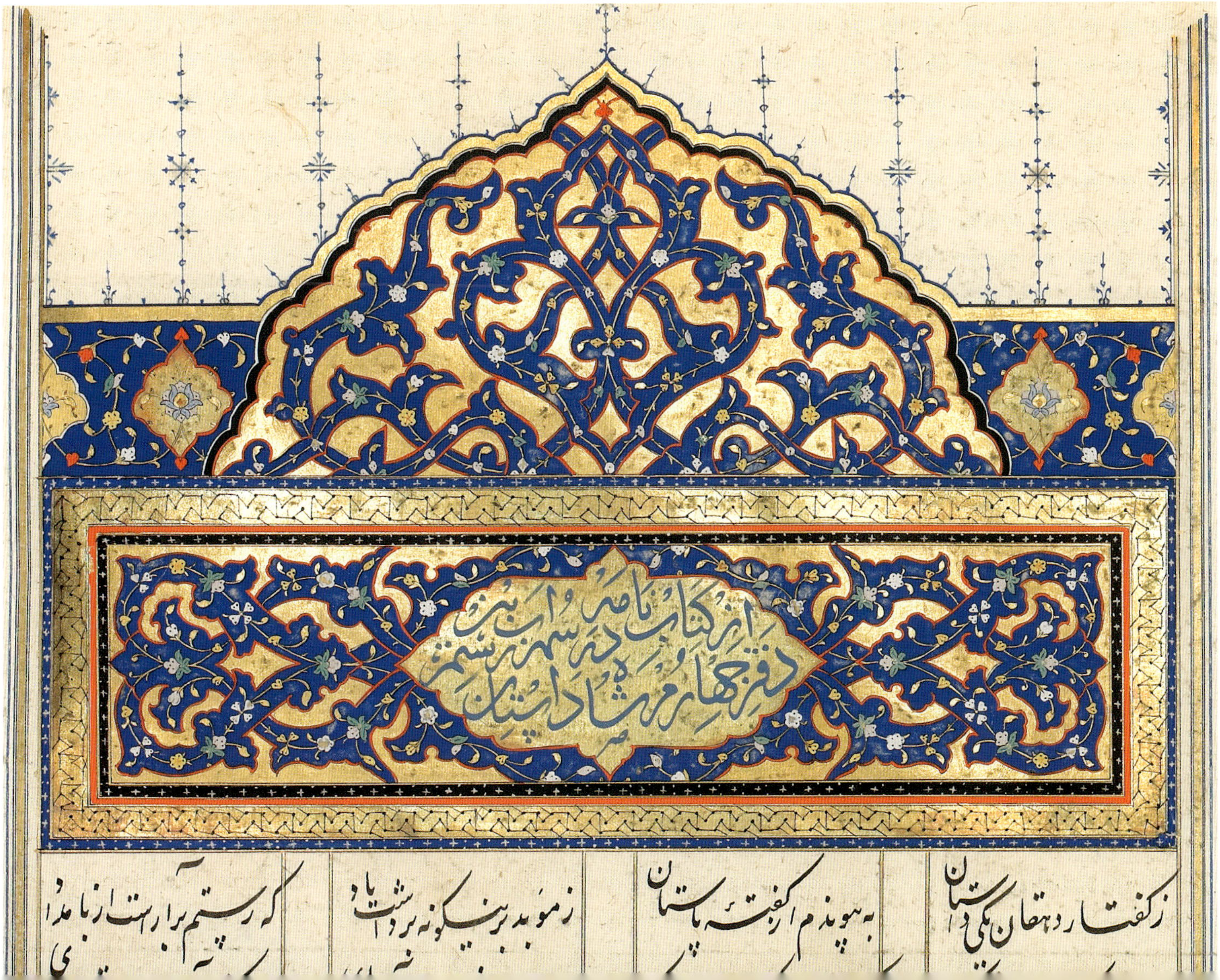

دفتر پنجم

دفتر پنجم در سنا اسکندرنامه

سکندر چو بر تخت بنشست گفت   که با جان شاهان خرد باد جفت
که پیروز گر در جهان ایزد است   جهاندار گر زو نترسد بد است

دفتر چهارم

ارکان ثانی ابر دفتر چهارم ارشاد است

ز گفتار دهقان یکی ...ستان   به موبد بر این که سر پرستان   از موبد بر این است برابر با مدا
که رستم برابر است با مدا

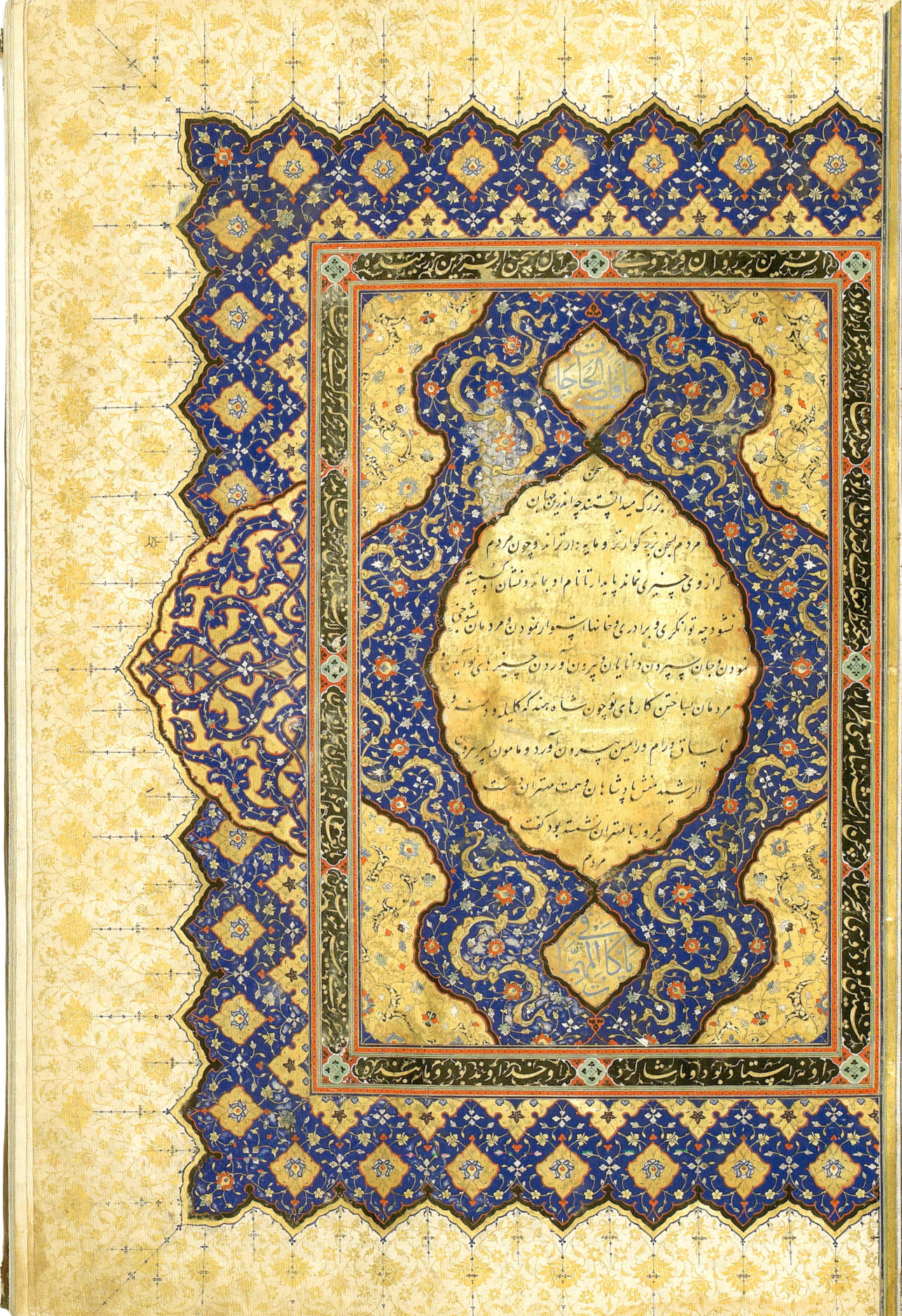

The illuminated frontispiece, ff. 1v–2r

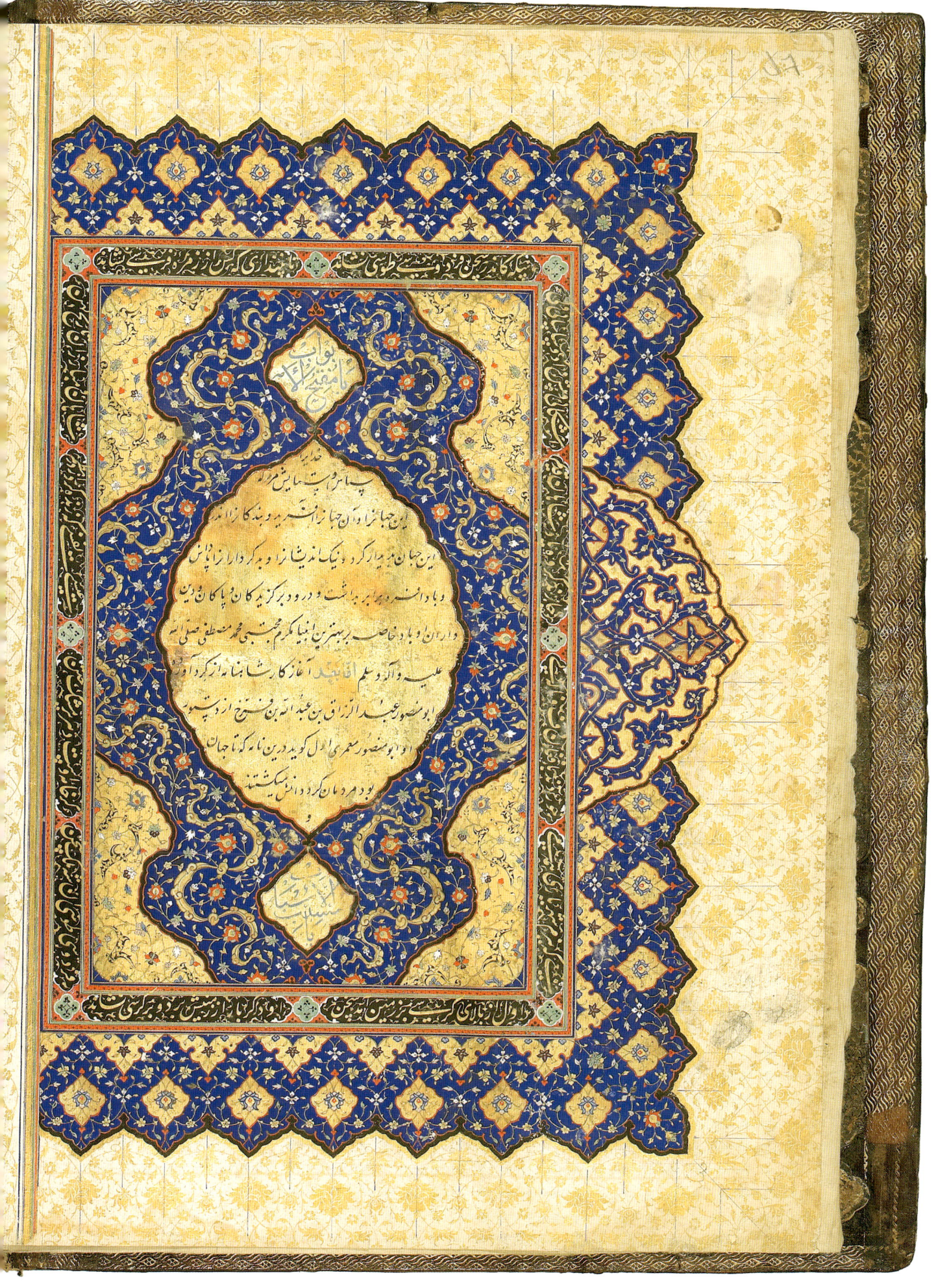

gold cable, though the colours of the marginal rules alternate between any combination of orange, turquoise, black and blue. The marginal rules are also frequently dotted with white, black or red, so that they appear like continuous chains. The central panel is surmounted by a border, which may be smooth (*e.g.* f. 75v), or lobed and containing rows of gold palmettes (*e.g.* f. 149v) like the border of the frontispiece. The upper border is frequently broken by a projecting triangular device, either identical to the *hasps* on the frontispiece and containing the same pattern of blue intertwining tendrils (*e.g.* f. 371v; see page 31) or made up of a series of blue palmettes arranged in an arc on a gold ground (*e.g.* f. 299v). Scrolls of gold-stemmed pink, white, blue, orange, turquoise and yellow flowers fill the interstices of the rectangular panel and upper border in each *'unvan*. Though the *'unvans* are assembled from a pool of shared features, great attention has been paid to ensure that exactly the same combination of features or colours is never repeated.

This attention to detail is in accordance with the overall care with which the manuscript has been arranged, so that the chapter headings always fall on the verso of the page. The final page of each chapter is filled with gold scrolls of lotus blossoms, and in one case a drawing in gold of a phoenix and a dragon in combat (f. 38r). The spacing of the text is controlled by the occasional placing of the verses diagonally across the page, usually in anticipation of an illustration or at the end of a chapter, where the scribe wishes to draw the intention of the reader to the importance of the narrative (see illustration on page 30).[13]

Stylistically, the illumination on the frontispiece shares much with high-quality Iranian illumination of the second half of the sixteenth century. A useful comparison is with the illumination added in the sixteenth century to a Qur'an page copied by Yaqut al-Musta'simi, now in the Topkapı Palace Museum (fig. 2). It has been suggested that the page may have been illuminated in Iran and brought to the Ottoman court, as the style of the illumination is closer to the Safavid imperial style than the Ottoman.[14] With this page the illumination in the Eckstein *Shahnama* shares the outsize projecting *hasp* filled with blue tendrils, the lobed border, the bands of quatrefoils, and the thick gold cabling, dotted chains and gold cartouches mentioned above in connection with the frontispiece and *'unvans*. One might be tempted to conclude, from the illumination, that a Safavid origin was more likely than an Ottoman one.

However, as in the case of all the apparently Iranian elements in the Eckstein *Shahnama*, a process of adaptation is evident. For example, while the blue tendrils found on the *hasps* of the frontispiece are a common feature of Safavid illumination, and were occasionally used in Persian painting for the depiction of textiles (as in some of the tents in a painting from the *Haft Aurang* in the Freer Gallery; fig. 1),[15] the extension of the pattern to the central panel of some of the *'unvans* is extremely unusual and displays a degree of experimentation one would not expect of an Iranian manuscript of this period. The same can be said of the colour scheme for much of the illumination: though orange, turquoise and black are prominent in Safavid illumination and painting of the late sixteenth century, there is an overemphasis on these colours in some of the illumination that borders on the eccentric (*e.g.* ff. 252v, 299v, 371v, 561v; see pages 25 and 31).

There is nothing, however, about the illumination in the Eckstein *Shahnama* that we would recognise as particularly Ottoman. The overall impression given by the illumination is that the illuminator sought to copy Iranian models, but, owing either to freedom of expression or to lack of familiarity, experimented with these in a manner that was not quite Iranian. This hypothesis, as we shall see, is not at all inconsistent with an analysis of the paintings.

The Paintings

The following scenes are illustrated in the Eckstein *Shahnama*.

1. Firdausi and the poets of Ghazna (f. 5r)
2. Gayumarth enthroned (f. 11v; illustrated on page 44)
3. Faridun brings Zahhak to Mount Damavand (f. 22v; detail illustrated on page 62)
4. Salm and Tur murder Iraj (f. 29v; illustrated on page 40)
5. Sam kills the wizard Zand (f. 50v; detail illustrated on page 4)
6. Sam kills the gardener (f. 60r)
7. Sam kills the Faghfur of Chin (f. 72r; illustrated on page 45)
8. Sam asks the Simurgh to return Zal (f. 77v; illustrated on page 46)
9. The birth of Rustam (f. 95r)
10. Rustam lifts Afrasiyab by the belt (f. 110r; see page 42)
11. Rustam's seventh labour: he kills the White Div (f. 119v; illustrated on page 13)
12. Kay Ka'us in his flying machine (f. 129v; see page 61)
13. Rustam discovers Suhrab's identity (f. 146r; see page 16)
14. Guruy executes Siyavush (f. 174v)
15. Giv kills Tazhav in revenge for the death of Bahram (f. 212v)
16. Rustam kills Ashkabus and his horse (f. 229v)

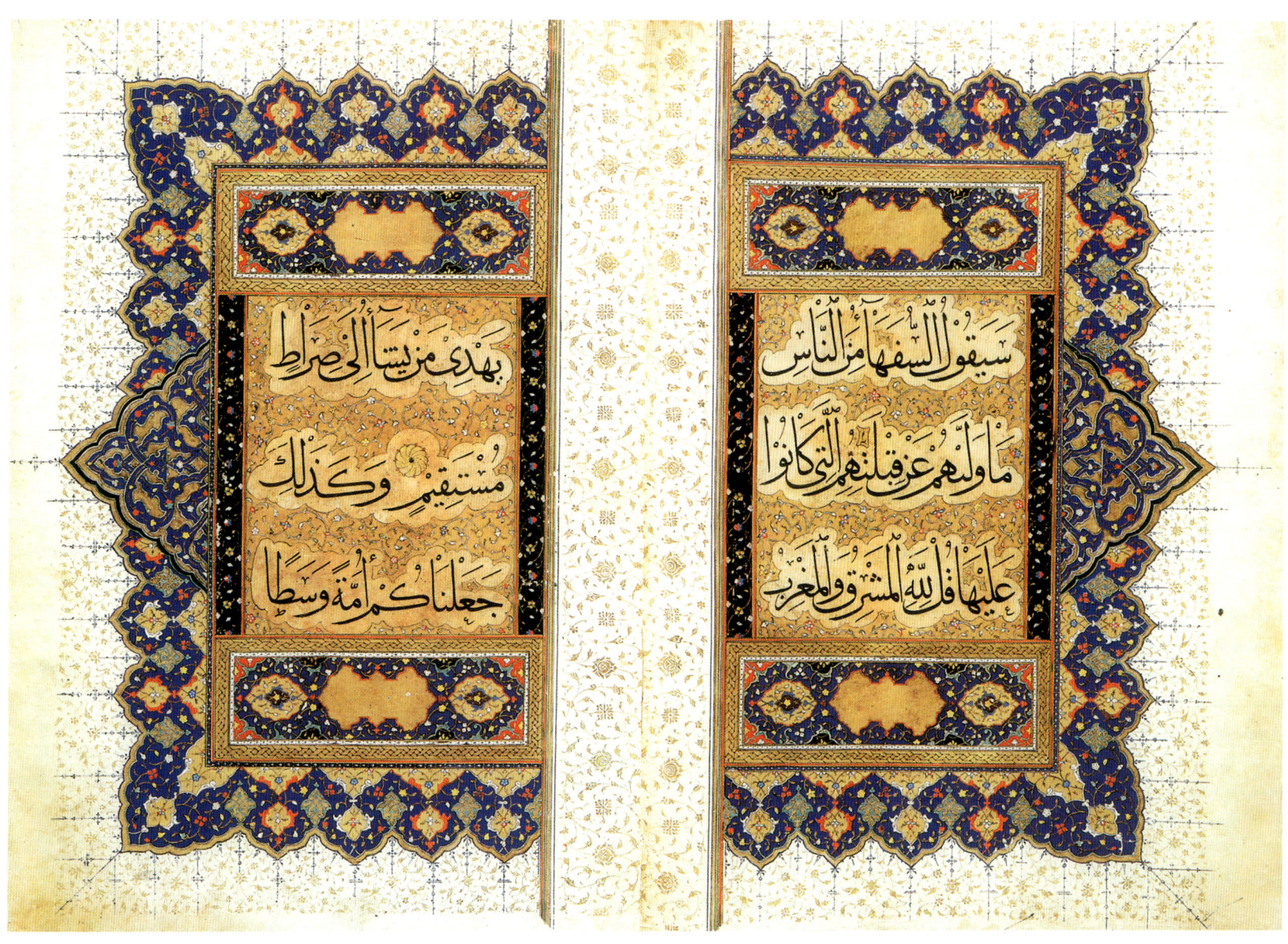

Fig. 2 Frontispiece from a Qur'an illuminated in the mid sixteenth century, Topkapı Saray Müzesi, Istanbul, TKS EH. 227, ff. 1v–2r

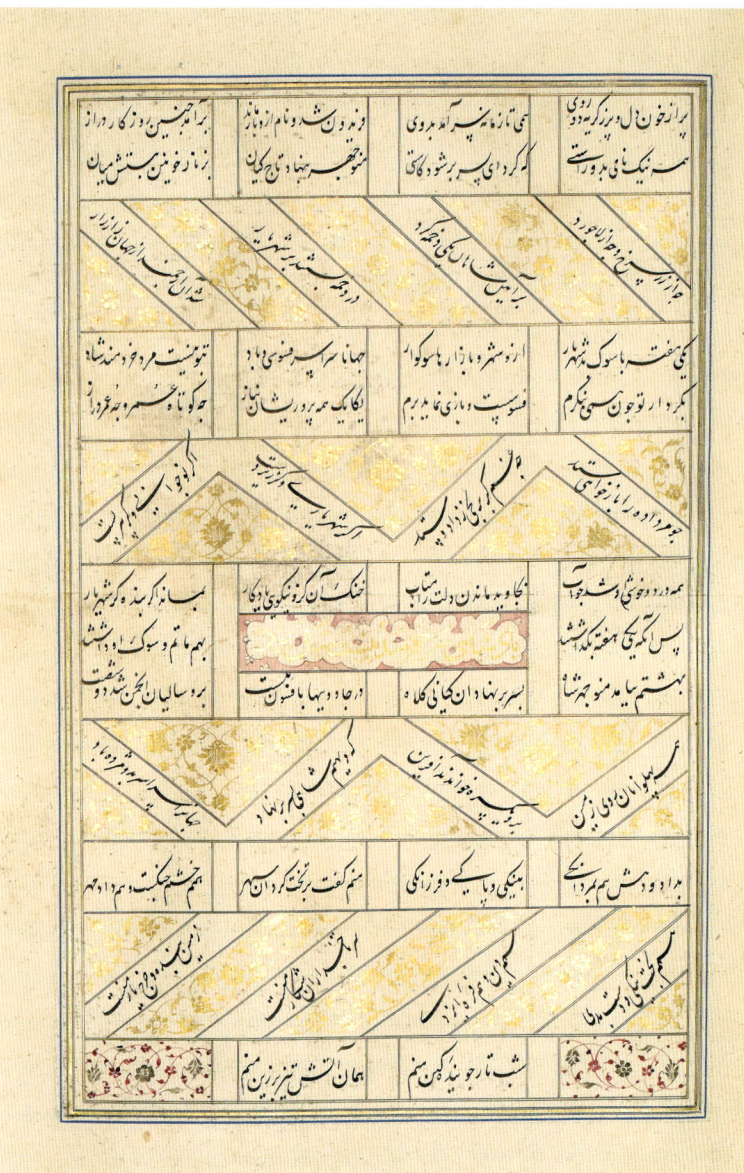

ABOVE Illuminated page, f. 37r

OPPOSITE ABOVE Illuminated chapter heading, f. 252v

OPPOSITE BELOW Illuminated chapter heading, f. 371v

17. Rustam pulls the Khaqan of Chin from his elephant (f. 240v; illustrated on page 43)
18. Akvan Div flings Rustam into the sea (f. 250v; see page 33)
19. Rustam rescues Bizhan from the pit (f. 267r)
20. Rustam is about to kill Barzu (f. 298r)
21. Bizhan kills Human (f. 309v)
22. The first combat: Fariburz kills Gulbad (f. 322v; detail illustrated on page 8)
23. Kay Khusrau throws Shida to the ground (f. 340r; illustrated on page 21)
24. The execution of Afrasiyab (f. 359v; illustrated on page 35)
25. Isfandiyar kills Bidarafsh (f. 390v; illustrated on page 6)
26. Isfandiyar kills Arjasp to rescue his sisters (f. 408r; illustrated on page 17)
27. Rustam shoots Isfandiyar in the eyes (f. 427r)
28. Bahman fights Humay (f. 453r; illustrated on page 14)
29. Bahman executes Faramurz (f. 499v)
30. A wrestling match between Azar and Sipah (f. 533r; illustrated on page 39)
31. Iskandar kills the Fur of Hind (f. 569r)
32. Iskandar dies in Babylon (f. 584r)

Like the other truncated *Shahnamas*, the Eckstein *Shahnama* contains illustrations that are clearly related to a group of manuscripts of *Qisas al-Anbiya'* (Stories of the Prophets) that were produced in the 1570s and 1580s, almost certainly in the Ottoman Empire. In her seminal article on the truncated *Shahnamas*, Karin Rührdanz noted the artistic continuity between the styles of painting in these and those of the Eckstein and other *Shahnamas*.[16] Like those in the *Qisas* series, the illustrations in the Eckstein *Shahnama* exhibit fairly consistent styles that nonetheless show variations from painting to painting. This phenomenon has been related to the commercial origins of the manuscripts, and was probably the result of a situation in which different ateliers or workshops collaborated on a single manuscript.[17]

Two main distinct styles can be discerned, both of them in some way related to the styles found in the *Qisas* series. Analysis of these corroborates the theory that ateliers and not individual artists were responsible for the pictorial cycle of the Eckstein *Shahnama*. The grouping of the artists into ateliers would explain the continuity in styles between the *Qisas* and *Shahnama* series, while also allowing for further developments and the absorption of other influences within a given atelier.

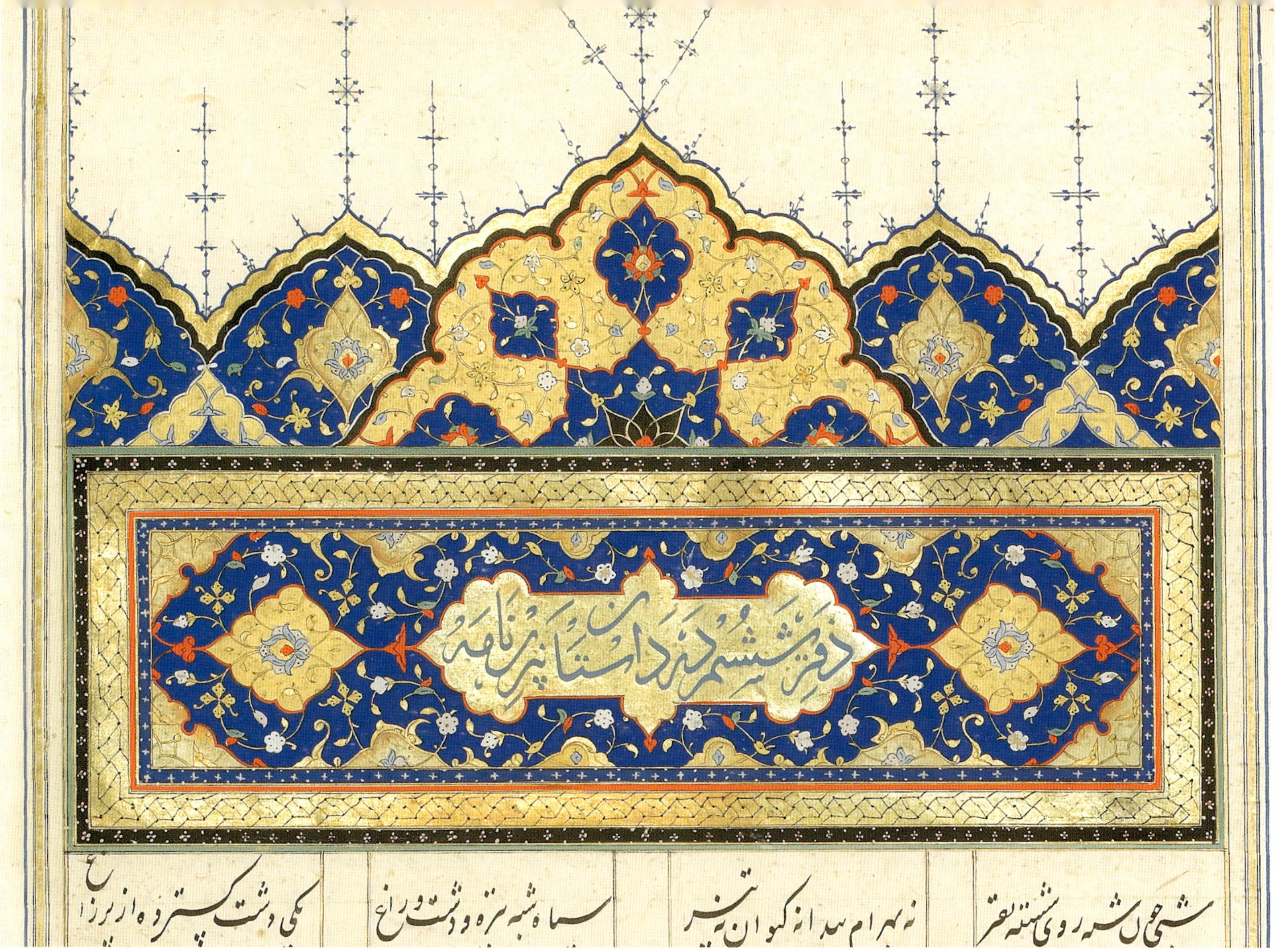
دفتر ششم در داستان بیژن نامه
شبی چون شبه روی شسته بقیر
نه بهرام پیدا نه کیوان نه تیر
سپاه شبه تیره بر دشت و راغ
یکی دشت گسترده از پر زاغ

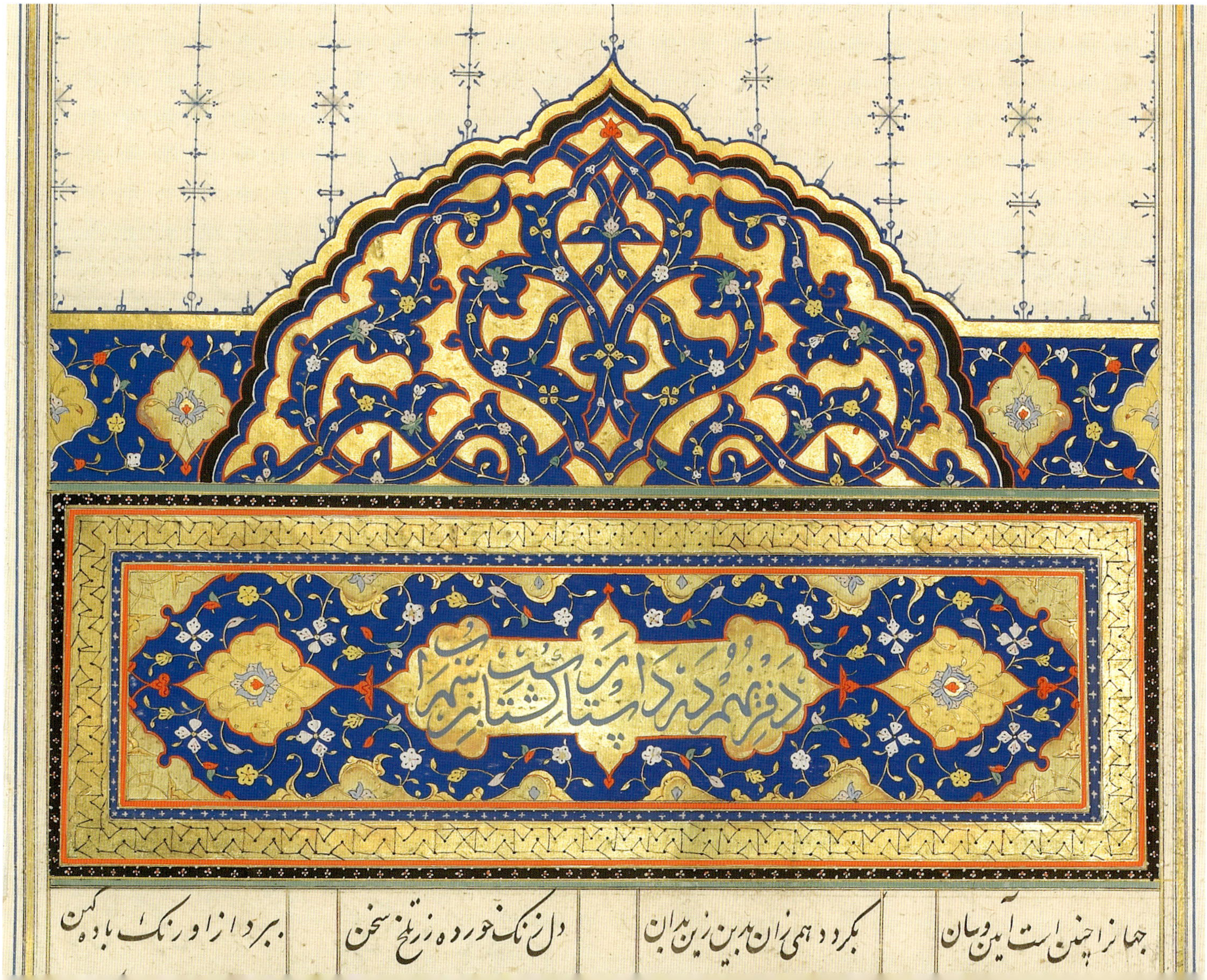
دفتر نهم در داستان گشتاسب شاه
جهانرا چنین است آیین و سان
بگردد همی زان بدین زین بدان
دل زنگ خورده ز تلخ سخن
ببرد از او زنگ باده کهن

Akvan Div flings Rustam into the sea, no. 18, f. 250v

A ferocious demon, Akvan Div, had been harassing the horsemen of Iran and eating their herds. The huge demon came across the hero Rustam, who had been sent to eliminate the menace, asleep on the ground. Tearing up the earth on which the hero was lying, Akvan Div lifted Rustam in the air and cast him into the sea. Once again, however, a combination of cunning and strength enabled Rustam to eventually overcome this fierce opponent.

The Styles

1 The first style (paintings nos. 1, 13, 18, 20–32)

One of the most intriguing and profound of the influences mentioned above is found in the sixteen paintings of the Eckstein *Shahnama* (not including the six detached paintings) executed in what appears to be the Qazvin court style of the late sixteenth century. The illustrations in this style have been cautiously identified as the work of 'Ali Asghar, one of the major Safavid court artists who worked in the ateliers of Shah Tahmasp, Sultan Ibrahim Mirza and Shah Isma'il II, and was the father of the famous painter and draughtsman Riza 'Abbasi.[18] The apparent discrepancy in style between these paintings and the others in the *Shahnama* has led to the suggestion that work on the Eckstein *Shahnama* began in Qazvin and was then completed elsewhere.[19] But before discussing how these paintings came to be included in the Eckstein *Shahnama*, it is worthwhile outlining the characteristics peculiar to this style.

One of the most marked features of the paintings in the 'Ali Asghar-esque style is a distinctive treatment of the rocks in the background, which are frequently drawn in soft lilac and mauve streaks. In general, great attention is paid to the composition of the rocks, and in the most visually arresting of the illustrations in the Eckstein *Shahnama* the artist has invested in them an energy that echoes the main action. In *Akvan Div flings Rustam into the sea* (no. 18; illustrated opposite), it is almost as if the rocks themselves were propelling the demon into the air. The wild energy of this painting is enhanced by the presence of a snarling lion and a tiger on either side of the main action; the line running from the taut concave back of the crouching tiger on the left to the convex arched back of the lion on the right creates a wave of movement like the sudden release of tension that propels the giant demon into the air. In the bottom right corner two naturalistically rendered foxes weave between the rocks and the margin of the page, their agitation adding to the general commotion.

Another feature common to the first style, and one associated with the work of 'Ali Asghar, is the rendering of figures in three-quarter view. This is used to particular effect in the illustration *The execution of Afrasiyab* (no. 24; see following page), where the lopped head of the Turanian king faces the ground in the opposite direction to the upturned face of his terrified fellow captive and brother Garsivaz. The effect here is to produce a steep and dizzying vertical axis that mirrors the confusion and terror of the captives. The rocks are also used to great effect in this illustration.

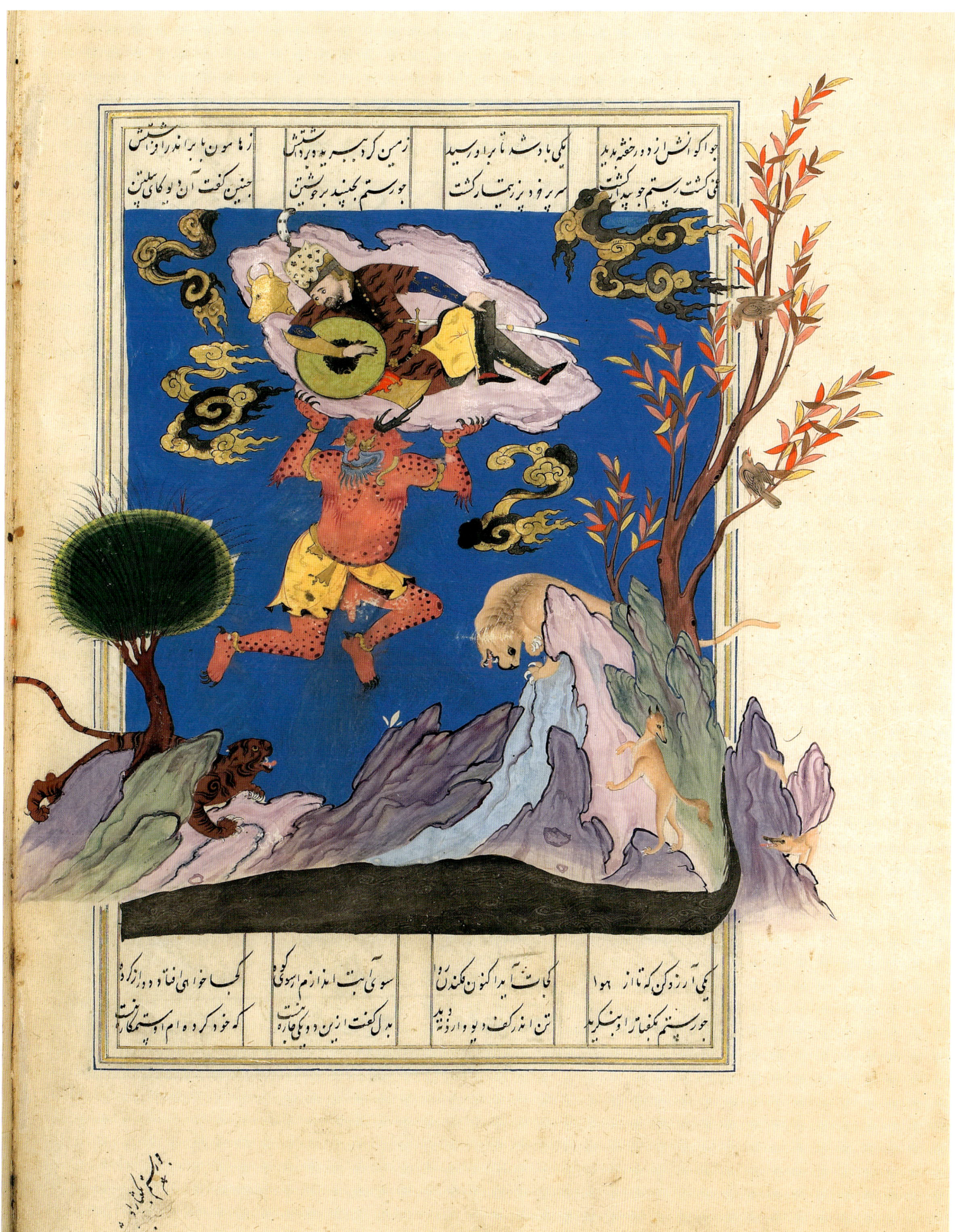

The execution of Afrasiyab, no. 24, f. 359v

Though the Iranians had defeated the Turanian army on several occasions, the cunning Turanian King Afrasiyab had always avoided capture. Finally, following a heavy defeat, Afrasiyab had sought refuge in a cave on a solitary mountainside, from which the Iranians succeeded in drawing him out by using his brother Garsivaz as bait. On hearing the cries of Garsivaz, who had been tied up in an ox-hide, Afrasiyab emerged from the cave, only to be seized. In this illustration the Iranian King Kay Khusrau beheads Afrasiyab with his own hand, while the terrified Garsivaz remains tied up beside him.

The artist or artists behind this style also seem to have been fond of particular facial types: young men are frequently depicted with sharp almond eyes, small lips and slightly rounder faces (*e.g.* nos. 22, 28; see pages 8, 14), whereas older men have bonier faces, slightly crooked noses and pointed beards (*e.g.* nos. 23, 25; see pages 21, 6). Profiles of strong, almost grotesque faces with large bent noses also feature in many of the paintings of this style (*e.g.* no. 20), as do profiles of young men with rather weak chins (*e.g.* nos. 28, 29, 32; see page 14). There is also an abundance of finely dressed pages and attendants in floppy and feathered hats (*e.g.* nos. 23, 28; see pages 21, 14). The horses are slight, with small ears, and are on occasions, too, rendered in three-quarter view (*e.g.* no. 13; see page 37). Skies are generally painted in a thickly applied deep sky-blue with simplified Chinese-style clouds rendered in gold or grey. A pastel palette of salmon, lilac and grey-green is favoured for the painting of the landscape. As in Qazvin painting of the second half of the sixteenth century, the landscape often freely spills into the margin. Spindly, often leafless bushes dot the landscape and also frequently extend into the space beyond the margin (*e.g.* nos. 18, 22; see previous page).

It is important to note that more than one artist was certainly involved in these paintings. While all of the illustrations in this style are finely painted, some lack the compositional imagination evident in such miniatures as *Akvan Div flings Rustam into the sea* or *The execution of Afrasiyab*. While these other illustrations share many of the distinct facial types and palette mentioned above, they nonetheless have a more routine feel to them, such as one might expect in a commercially produced manuscript. Common to many of these is a fairly flat rocky backdrop with a level horizon, peopled by rows of figures of uniform facial type (*e.g.* nos. 20, 29, 31).

Some of these miniatures are close in style to the work of an atelier responsible for the most Persian-looking illustrations in a series of *Qisas al-Anbiya'* manuscripts from the 1560s and 1570s. With the work of this atelier they share the tall slender figures with round heads on thin necks and a naturalistic but rather routine treatment of the landscape.[20] For this a possible explanation is that the atelier responsible for the Qazvin-style paintings in the *Qisas* series was also responsible for this group of illustrations, while the workshop style as a whole was influenced by the arrival of a new artist or artists, probably from Iran. The identification of this artist as 'Ali Asghar, however, was made on the basis of an examination of the six detached illustrations alone, before the truncated *Shahnamas* had even been identified as a group. Thirty years on, the

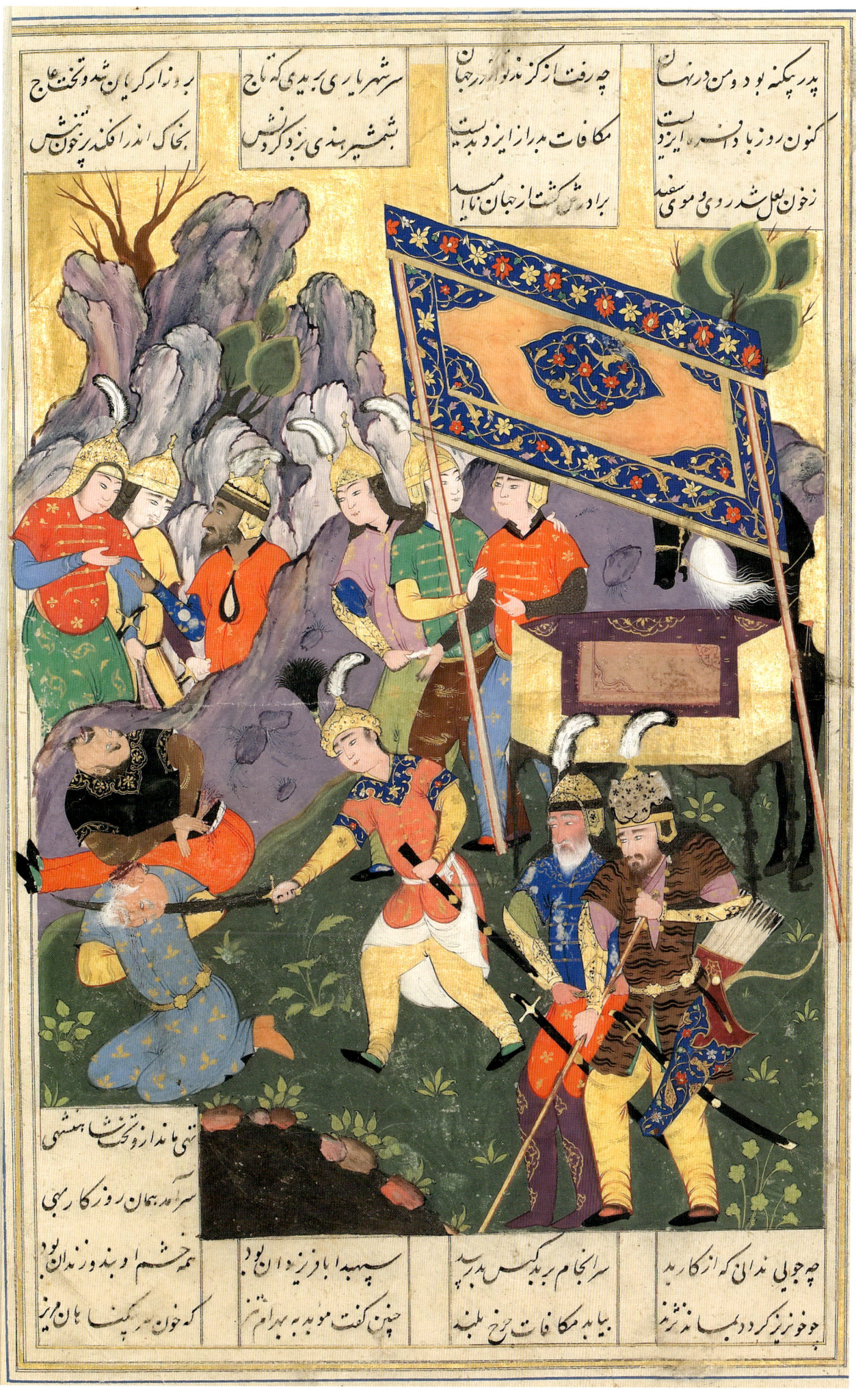

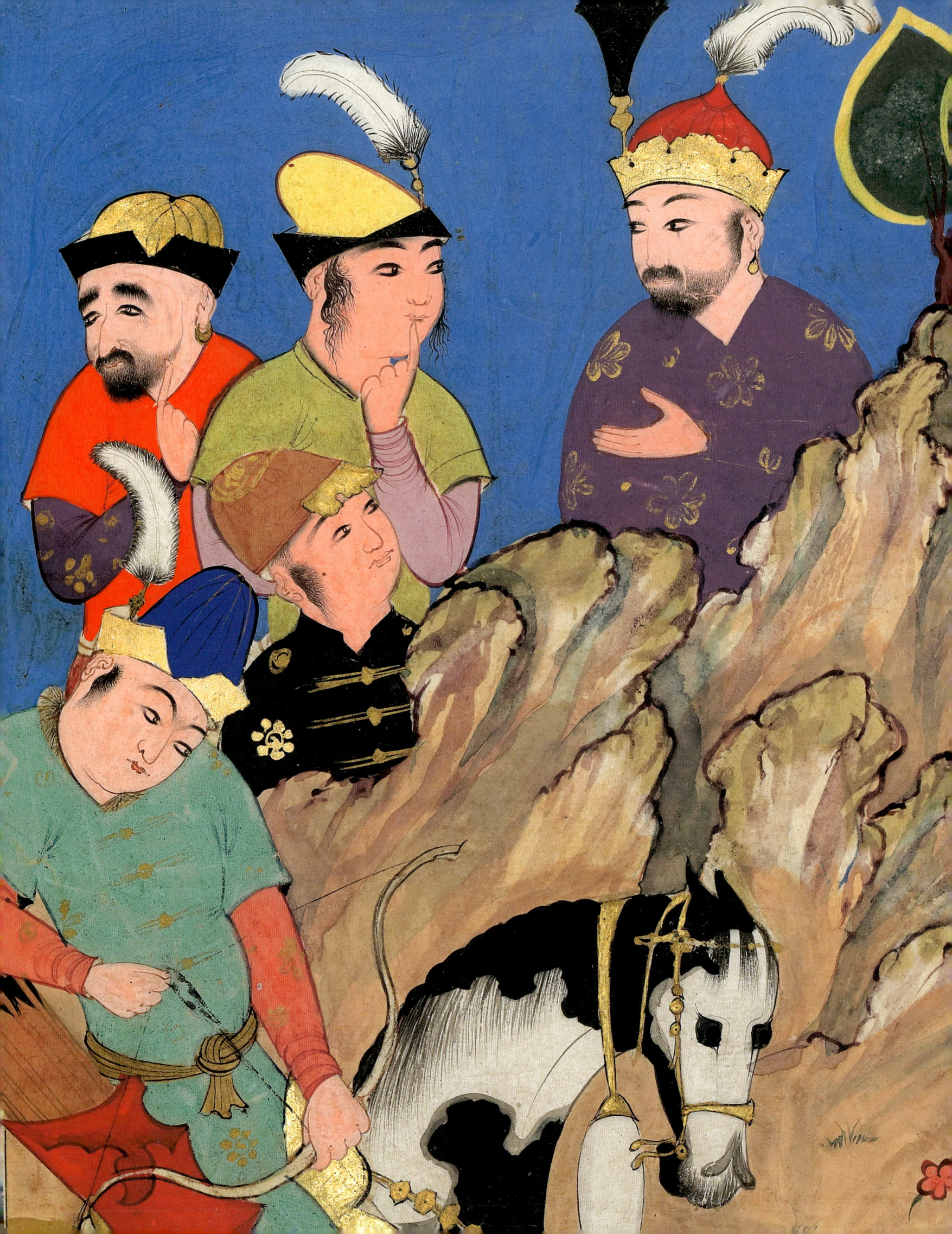

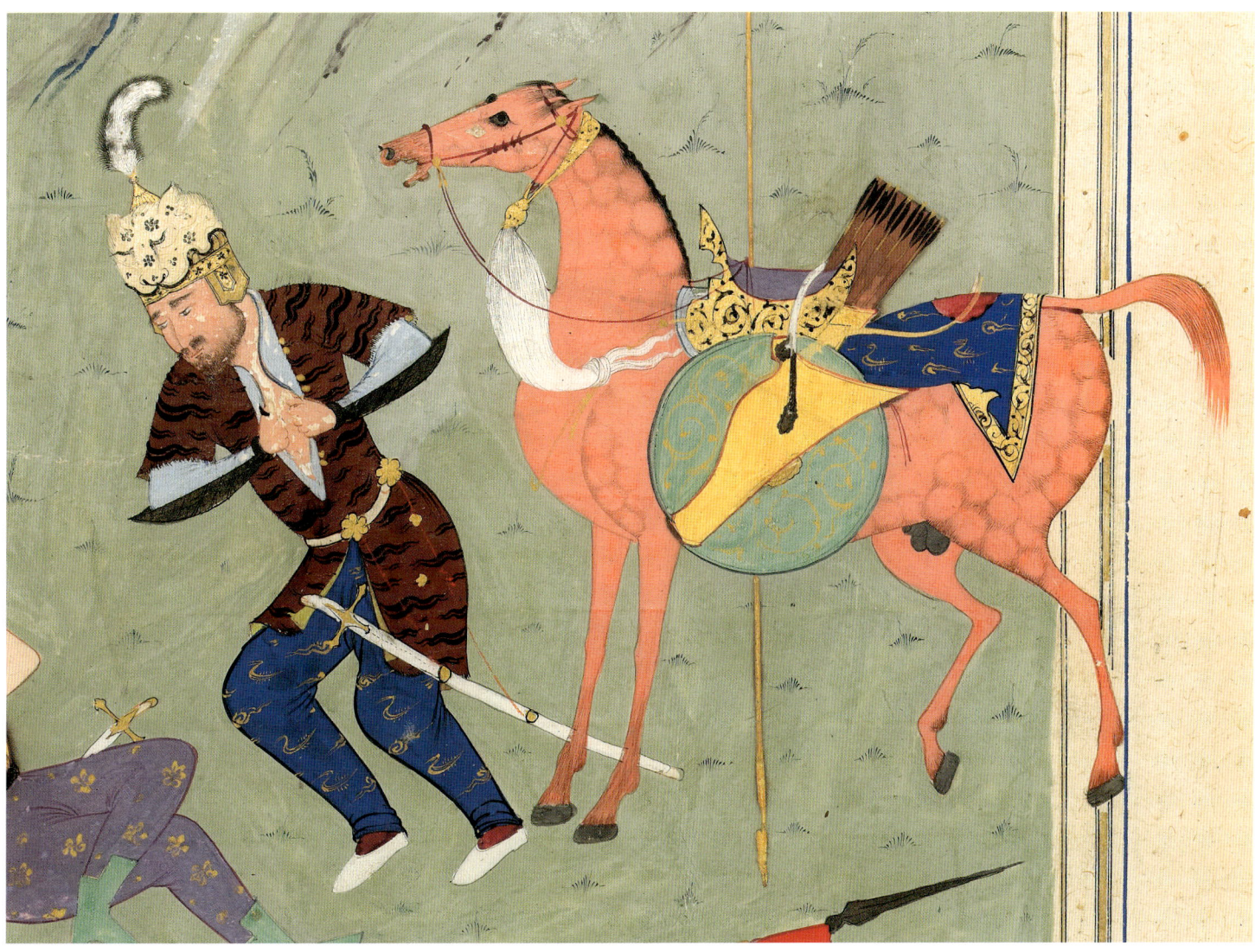

LEFT Detail from *Isfandiyar kills Bidarafsh*, no. 25, f. 390v

ABOVE Detail from *Rustam discovers Suhrab's identity*, no. 13, f. 146r

attribution seems less likely: 'Ali Asghar's whereabouts after the death of Shah Isma'il II in 1577 are not known, but if he had migrated to the Ottoman Empire contemporary sources would surely have mentioned it.[21] A more likely attribution would be to a pupil or pupils of his, which would explain the imprint of the master's work on the manuscript as well as the more general influence of the Shah Isma'il II *Shahnama*, a subject to which we will turn shortly.

This revised hypothesis would explain why the paintings in this style exhibit to varying degrees the characteristics of both the 'Ali Asghar-esque and the *Qisas* styles. Some paintings, such as *Akvan Div flings Rustam into the sea* (no. 18; see page 33) would seem to be in pure 'Ali-Asghar style, whereas *Bahman executes Faramurz* (no. 29) is much closer to the *Qisas* style. Most of the paintings in the 'first' style incorporate elements of both. In *A wrestling match between Azar*

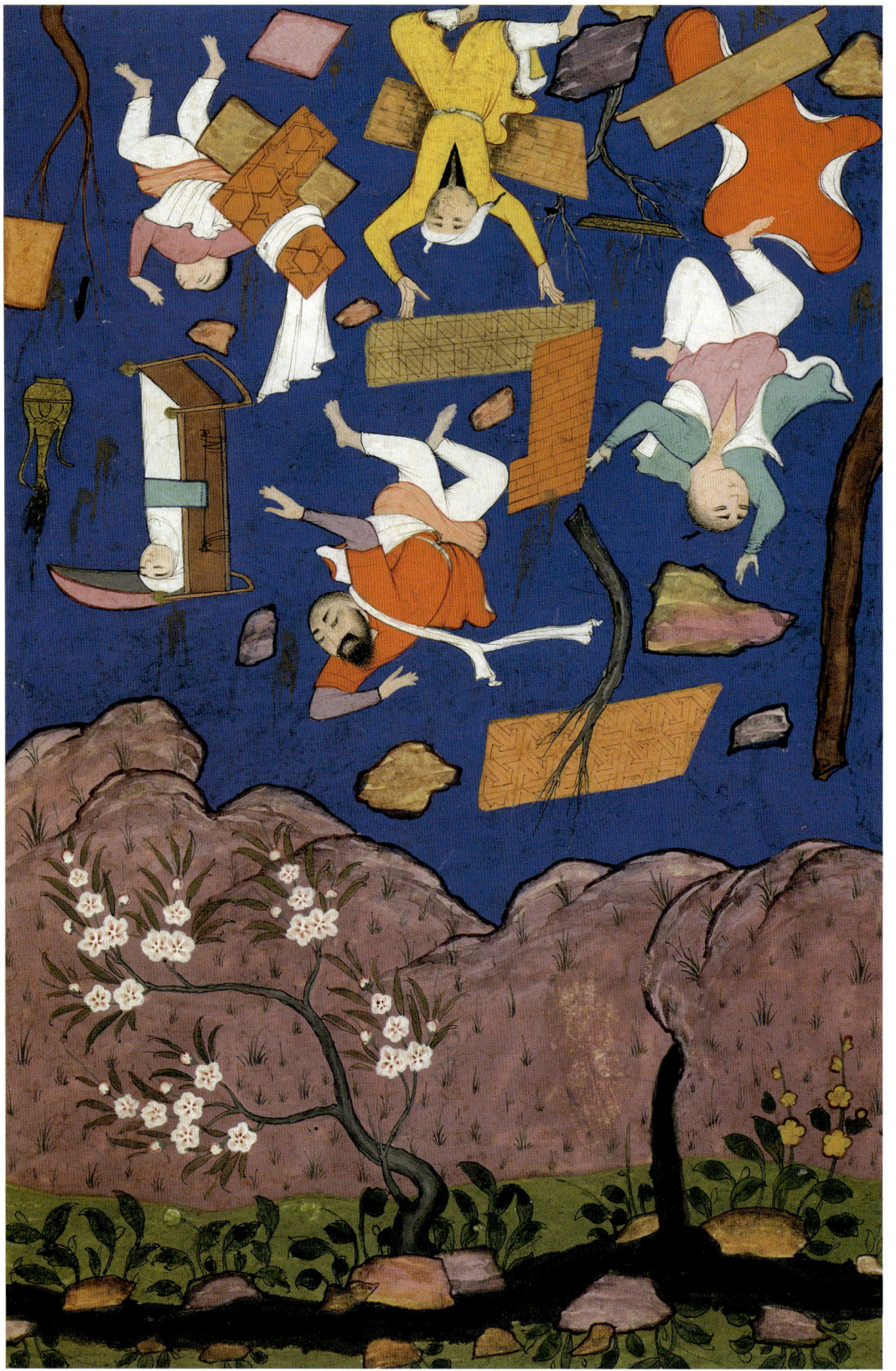

LEFT

Fig. 3 *The destruction of Sodom*, from *Qisas al-Anbiya'*, Staatsbibliothek zu Berlin, Preussicher Kulturbesitz, Berlin, Orientabteilung, Diez A fol. 3, f. 50v

The round faces and elongated bodies of the figures in this manuscript provide a link with some of the paintings in the first style in the Eckstein *Shahnama*, such as the wrestlers in *A wrestling match between Azar and Sipah*, f. 533r (right).

RIGHT

A wrestling match between Azar and Sipah, no. 30, f. 533r

In the *Bahmannama*, following the death of his father Isfandiyar at the hands of Rustam, Bahman seeks revenge on Rustam's descendants, including Rustam's grandson, Azar. Having defeated and executed Azar's father Faramurz and fought several battles with him, Bahman finally makes peace with Azar. Here Azar is engaged in a wrestling match with another hero, Sipah. While the bearded onlookers in this painting are reminiscent of the style of the court painter 'Ali Asghar, the tall, round-headed wrestlers recall some of the paintings in the *Qisas al-Anbiya'* series of manuscripts.

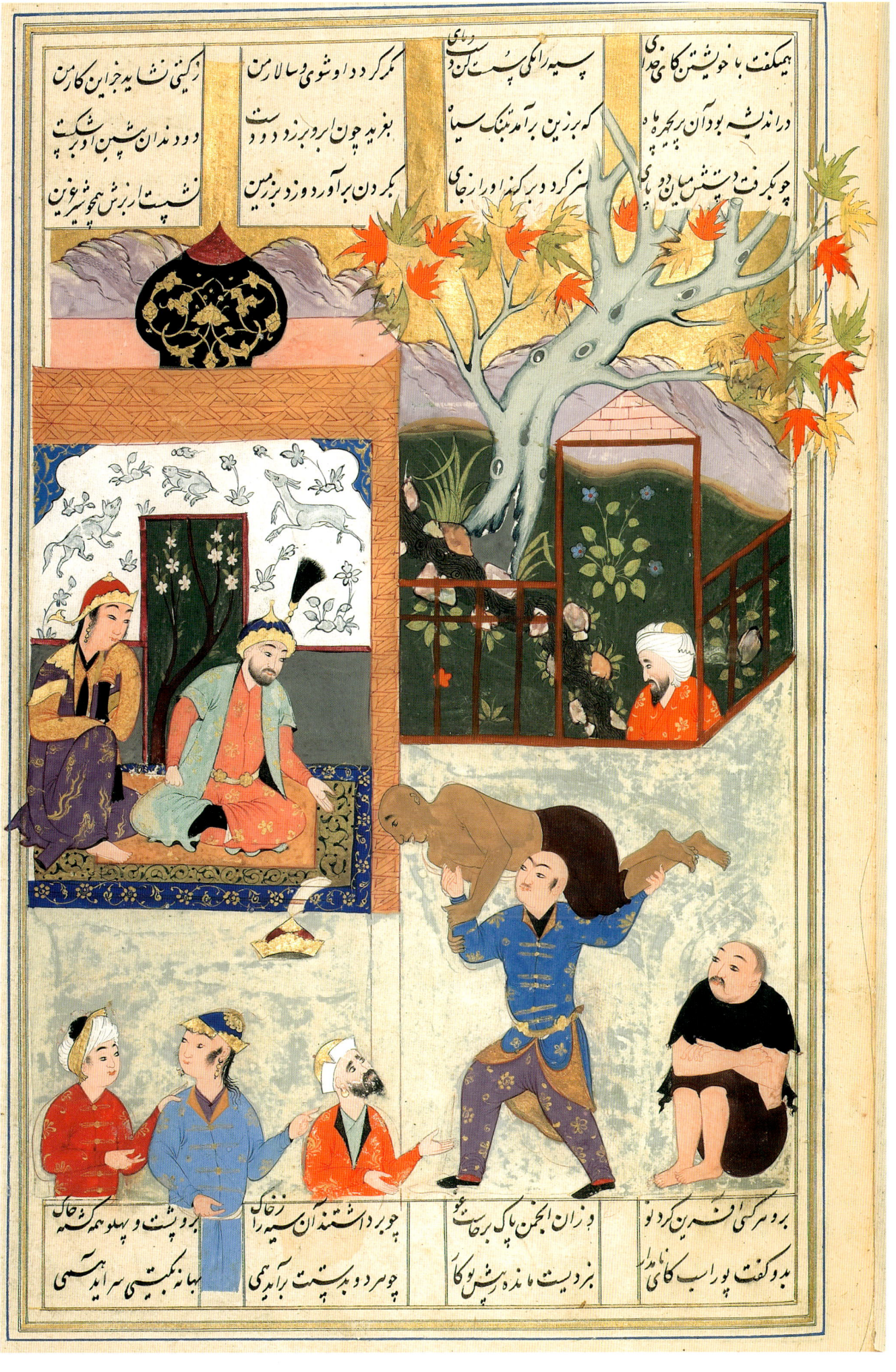

بخون برادر چه بندی کمر	چه سودی ز دل برگشته مدار	جهان جوینده یا فی خون ریز	کمن با جوانذار ریزو استین
همان خشم بودش ببان سرد	یکی خنجر از موزه بیرون کشید	سراپای او را در خون کشید	

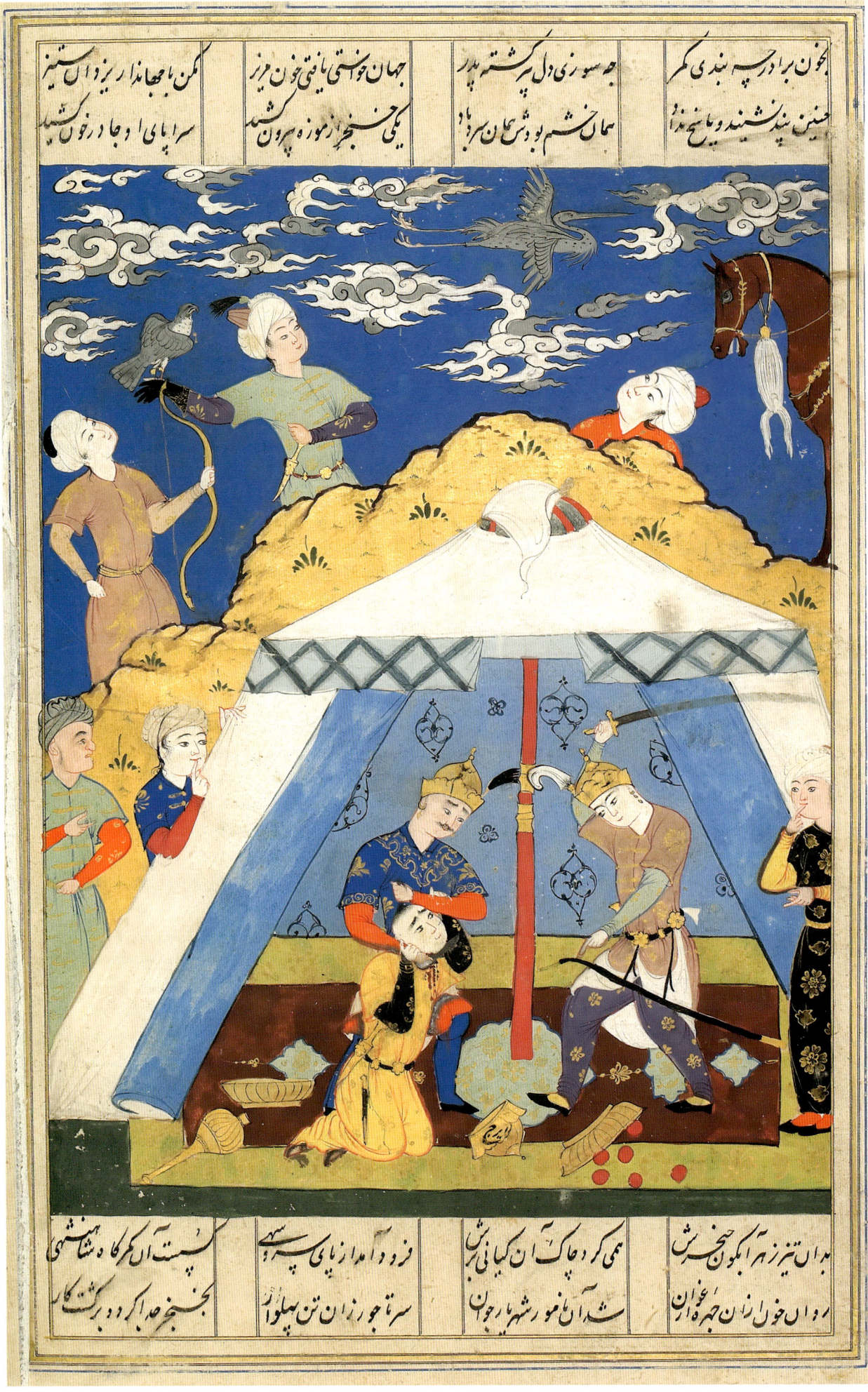

بدان تیز زهر آبکون خنجرش	همی کرد چاک آن کیانی بر	فرود آمد از پای آن سرو سهی	کست آل کمر گاه ببشتشی
روان خون از ان جبهٔ غیوان	شد آن ما فور شهیار جوان	سرتا جو زان تن شهریار جوان	الخنجر خدا کردو برکت کار

and Sipah (no. 30; see page 39), for example, the faces of the three bearded figures are typical of the style associated with 'Ali Asghar, whereas the three figures with their round shaved heads and almost identical expressions are very close to the *Qisas al-Anbiya'* style seen in an illustration of *The destruction of Sodom* (fig. 3).[22] That the two styles could be amalgamated so seamlessly could be explained by the common origins of both in the Qazvin court style.

II The second style (paintings nos. 2–4, 6–7, 9–12, 14–15, 17, 19)

Fourteen paintings in the Eckstein *Shahnama* display stylistic affinities with the so-called 'second style' from the *Qisas al-Anbiya* series, characterized by elongated figures with thin waists, conical necks and plump faces. With the second *Qisas* style these paintings also share a fondness for landscapes in thin pastel, especially lilac, washes, trees with crowns consisting of individually painted branches or leaves superimposed over a solid green circle, exuberant vegetation, and simple spatial arrangements whereby large figures are placed close to the picture plane along a horizontal axis. The sky in two of the paintings in the Eckstein *Shahnama* are rendered in the same distinctive blue and white streaks as in some of the paintings in the second *Qisas* style.[23]

Since the second *Qisas* style has been discussed authoritatively elsewhere, no introduction to it is needed here. However, it is worth repeating the observation that, while the second style clearly owes a debt to Iranian styles of painting of the second half of the sixteenth century, it is idiosyncratic enough to have led scholars to propose an Ottoman origin for it.[24] It should also be noted that this group of fourteen paintings in the Eckstein *Shahnama* show perhaps even greater stylistic variety than the *Qisas* paintings in the second style; given that the truncated *Shahnamas* are assumed to have grown out of the *Qisas* series and not the other way round, a degree of stylistic development would, after all, not be surprising.

It is also interesting to note that certain developments within the second style are restricted to certain paintings, and that paintings that share certain peculiarities are on the whole grouped together. Paintings nos. 3 and 4 (illustrated page 62 and opposite), for example, appear to be more spatially complex and more carefully executed than other paintings in the same group. The slighter figures, with their turbans wound higher on their heads in both paintings, and in particular the intense sky-blue and Chinese clouds in no. 4, *Salm and Tur murder Iraj*, would seem to indicate the influence of artists working in the first style. This hypothesis is strengthened by the iconographic connection between *Salm and Tur murder Iraj* and the *Shahnama* of Shah Isma'il II (see fig. 4). Though the depiction of

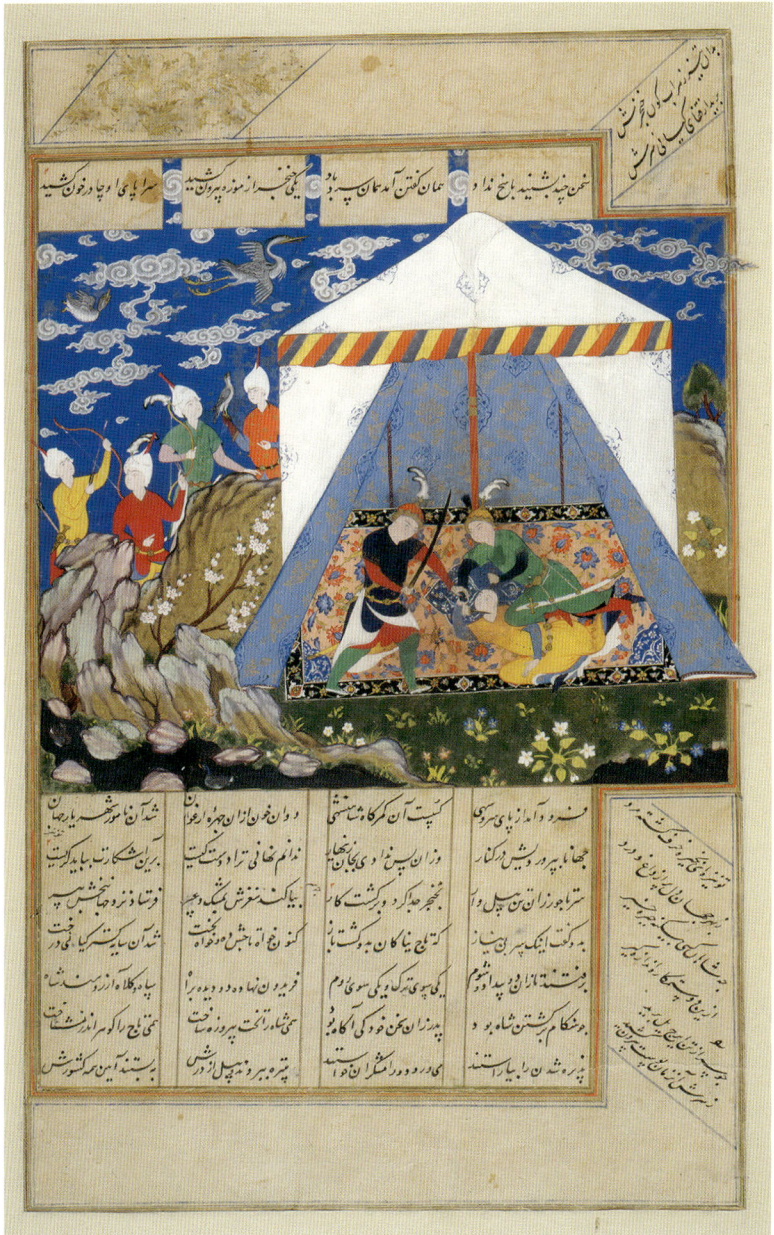

LEFT *Salm and Tur murder Iraj*, no. 4, f. 29v

King Faridun divided his realm between his three sons, Salm, Tur and Iraj. The two older brothers, however, considered Iraj to have been treated preferentially by their father and murdered him out of jealousy. The iconography of the scene is clearly based on the illustration of the same episode from the *Shahnama* of Shah Isma'il II, now in the Chester Beatty Library, Dublin (above).

ABOVE Fig. 4 *Salm and Tur murder Iraj*, from the *Shahnama* of Shah Isma'il II, Chester Beatty Library, Dublin, Per. 256, f. 3v

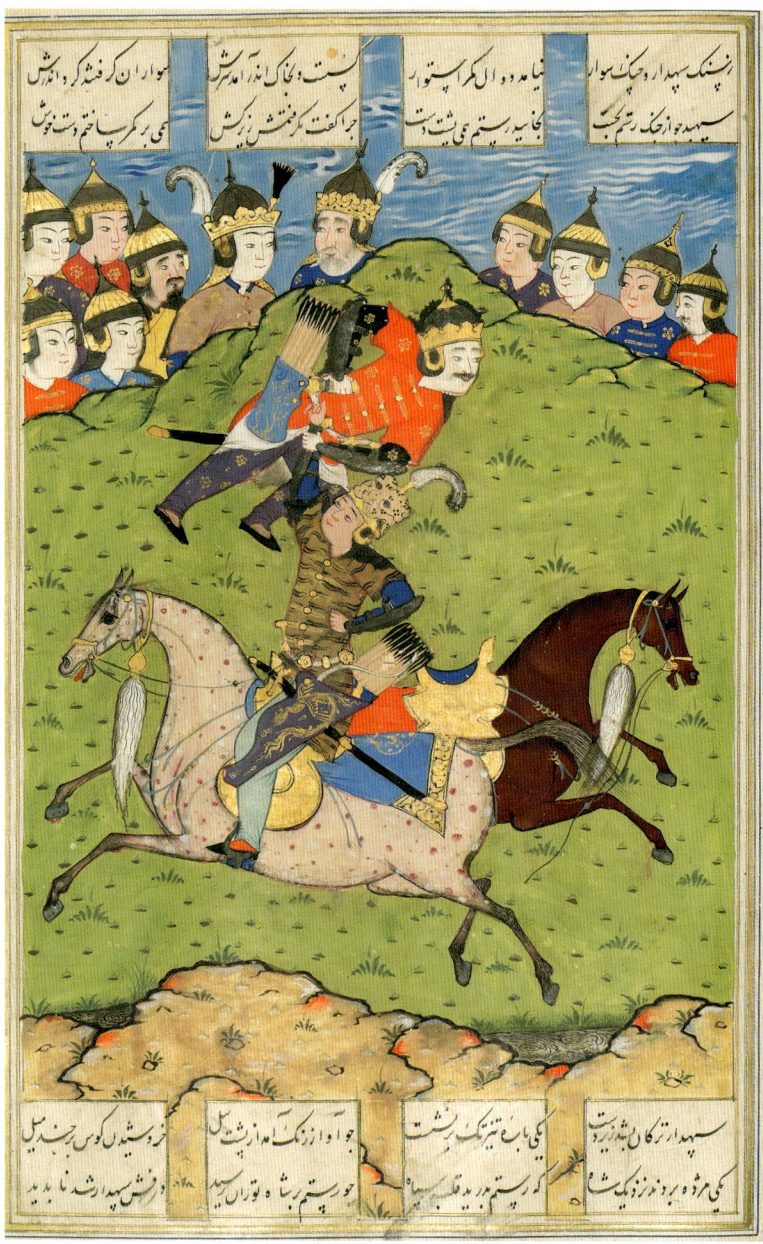

ABOVE *Rustam lifts Afrasiyab by the belt*, no. 10, f. 110r

The painting depicts a famous scene from a battle between the armies of Iran and the forces of Iran's main enemy, Turan. The hero Rustam, ignoring warnings of the strength of the Turanian king Afrasiyab, sought out the leader and lifted him from his horse by his belt.

RIGHT *Rustam pulls the Khaqan of Chin from his elephant*, no. 17, f. 240v

In the reign of Kay Khusrau Iran was faced with the challenge of an alliance between the Turanians and the Khaqan, or Emperor, of China. Enraged by the Khaqan's insults, Rustam lassoed him on the battlefield, pulling him down from his elephant.

this scene in a tent was not unknown by this period, there are other elements in the painting that are without doubt adapted from the illustration of the same scene in the Isma'il II *Shahnama*: the Chinese clouds, and the heron in the sky whose suggested fate in the claws of the falcon on the arm of the attendant on the horizon is meant to mirror the main action of the scene, all confirm that artists working on the Eckstein *Shahnama* were familiar with models from that manuscript.[25] Given the influence of the work of 'Ali Asghar on the first style of painting in the Eckstein *Shahnama* and the clear influence exercised by that style on *Salm and Tur murder Iraj*, it is perhaps surprising that the painter of the same scene in the Isma'il II *Shahnama* was not 'Ali Asghar, but rather another court artist, Murad al-Daylami.[26] The general imprint of that manuscript on the Eckstein *Shahnama* is unquestionable, however, and the confluence of features of the first style and the borrowing of iconography from the Isma'il II *Shahnama* is evidence enough that the Eckstein *Shahnama* was conceived as a single project under an overall direction and was carried out by artists familiar with the models and styles of Qazvin court painting of the 1570s.

Different, but nonetheless probably the work of artists from the same atelier, are a group of paintings that are somehow the most 'Turkish' of the illustrations. In common with paintings both from the *Qisas* series and contemporary Ottoman manuscripts, the figures and landscapes are large and boldly painted and the spatial arrangements simple, as though the aim were to illustrate the narrative in the most direct manner possible. The facial types and postures of the figures are similar to those in the first group of the second style that we have just considered, although on the whole the figures are larger and closer to the plane of the page. Some of the figures' large, oblong faces resemble those of the Ottoman court style of the 1580s and 1590s (especially nos. 9, 10; see this page). The horses are painted in the same manner as in *Salm and Tur murder Iraj*, with diamond eyes and open 'laughing' mouths, but are larger in size and more simply executed, so that piebald coats have come to be represented by almost childlike dots (*e.g.* no. 11; see page 13). The artist(s) responsible for this style is also fond of showing figures with their hands resting either on the frame of the painting or on the shoulder of a companion (*e.g.* nos. 5, 9, 12; see page 61). It should be noted that, as in the case of the first style, divisions between different groups of paintings within a particular style are not absolute, many paintings containing features of both; in *Sam kills the Faghfur of Chin* (no. 7; see page 45), for example, the smallish, thin-waisted figures hark back to the first group, whereas the simpler

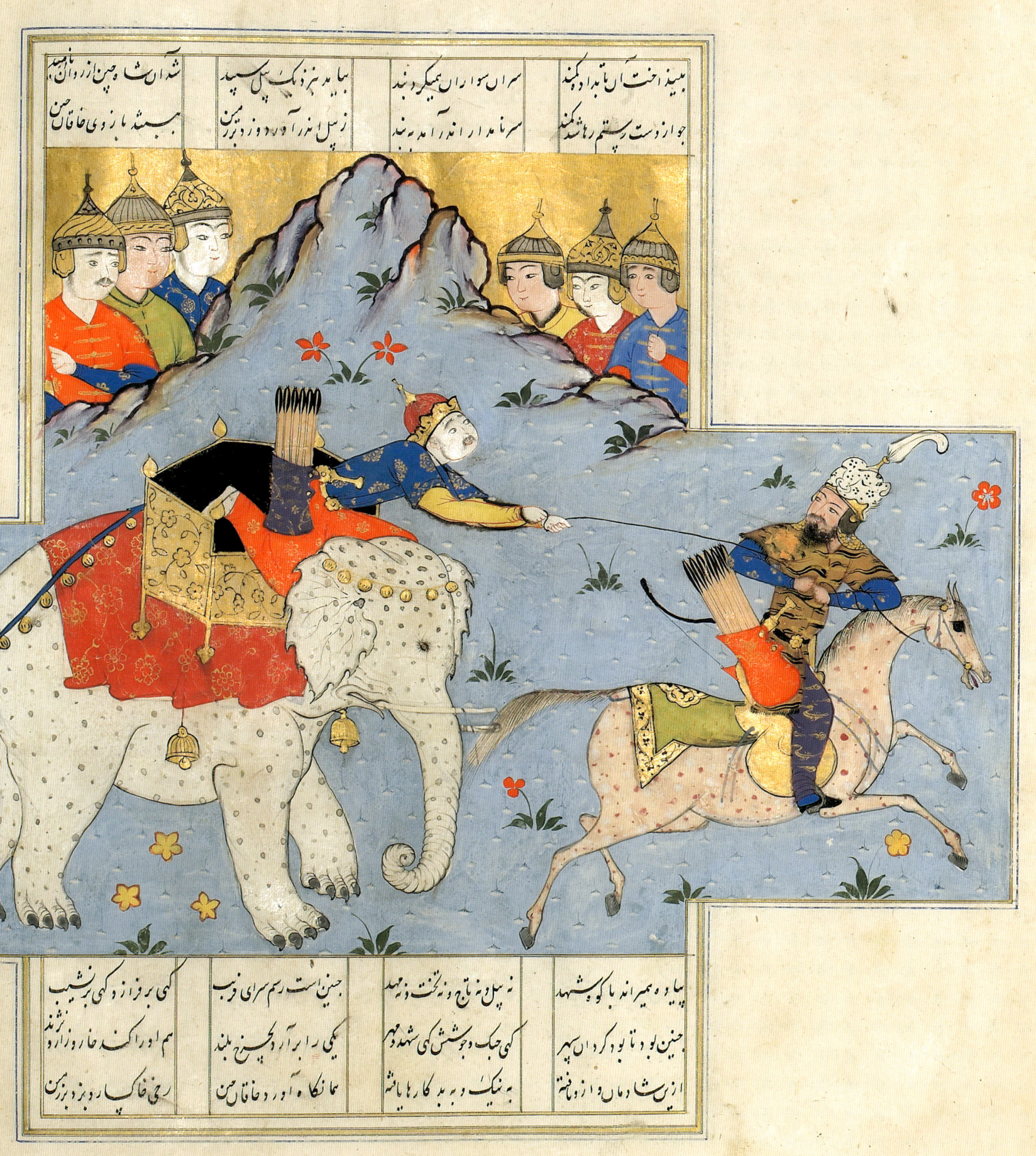

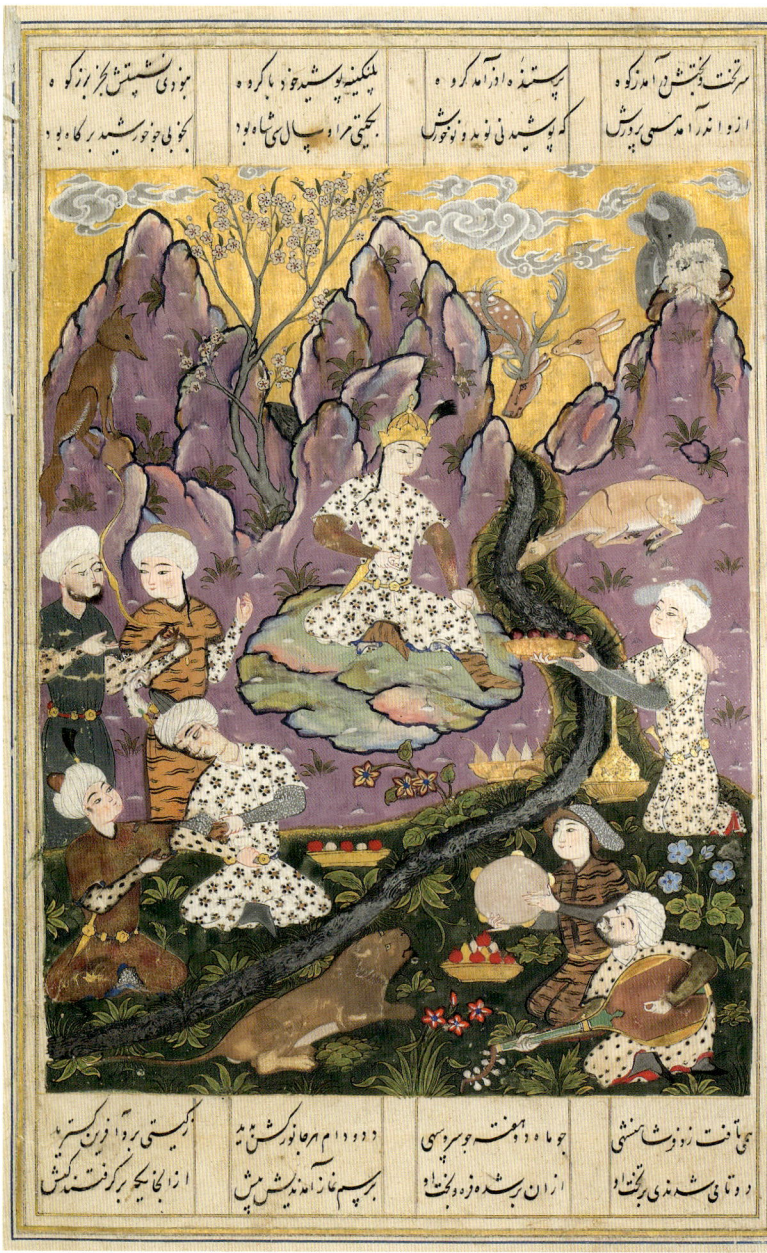

ABOVE *Gayumarth enthroned*, no. 2, f. 11v

Here the first King of Iran, Gayumarth, is seen holding court atop a mountain. In Gayumarth's time, until the invasion of Iran by the Black Demon, the son of Ahriman, the evil principle in the Mazdean tradition, men and animals lived in harmony.

RIGHT *Sam kills the Faghfur of Chin*, no. 7, f. 72r

The *Samnama*, one of the post-*Shahnama* epics most frequently interpolated into Firdausi's text, narrates the adventures of Sam, the King of Sistan and grandfather of Rustam, the bravest of all *Shahnama* heroes. Here Sam is seen slaying one of Iran's perennial enemies, the Emperor of China.

arrangement, rougher treatment of the landscape and striped sky place the painting in the second group. Again, it can be proposed that such variations within a clearly defined style were the result of the collaboration of different artists within a single atelier.

Two further paintings (nos. 14, 15) share the basic figural type common to all the paintings in this style, but stand apart owing to the even larger size of the figures, who are even closer to the picture plane. The heads of these figures are exaggeratedly large and round, to the point that they resemble those of the figures in the famous 'Big Head' *Shahnama* of the late fifteenth century. The skies in the two paintings are both painted in gold and the landscapes are rendered with light pastel washes and simple, large red flowers. Further evidence for the theory that different artists worked on the same painting can be found in *Rustam pulls the Khaqan of Chin from his elephant* (no. 17; see previous page); in this painting the smaller figures of Rustam and the Khaqan belong to the artist responsible for the other 'elephant' scene, *Sam kills the Faghfur of Chin* (see opposite page), whereas the gold sky, pastel-blue ground and row of big-headed figures in the background are clearly the work of the artist(s) of nos. 14 and 15.

Another picture (no. 2; see this page) sharing most of the features of the second style is distinguished by the sharp almond eyes and particularly child-like faces of the figures. These features are found, however, in illustrations from *Qisas* manuscripts painted in the second *Qisas* style, most clearly in a codex in the Bibliothèque nationale in Paris.[27]

III Other styles (paintings nos. 5, 8, 16)

While most of the paintings in the Eckstein *Shahnama* fall into one of the first two styles mentioned above, a handful of illustrations are more difficult to place. One of these, *Sam kills the wizard Zand* (no. 5, f. 50v), shares with paintings in the second style the simple spatial arrangement and straightforward approach to illustration, but the sharp, pointed beards of the figures along the horizon, the distinctive streaky treatment of the landscape, and the single outsize poppy plant constitute some of the hallmarks of the atelier responsible for the 'third style' in the *Qisas* manuscripts. These features find their clearest comparisons in a truncated *Shahnama* dated 1580, now in All Souls College, Oxford.[28]

The depiction of *Rustam kills Ashkabus* (no. 16) on first sight appears to be unconnected to any of the other styles in the manuscript; Rustam's distinctive blue horse, however, is clearly by the same hand that painted the horse in *Sam asks the Simurgh to return Zal* (no. 8).

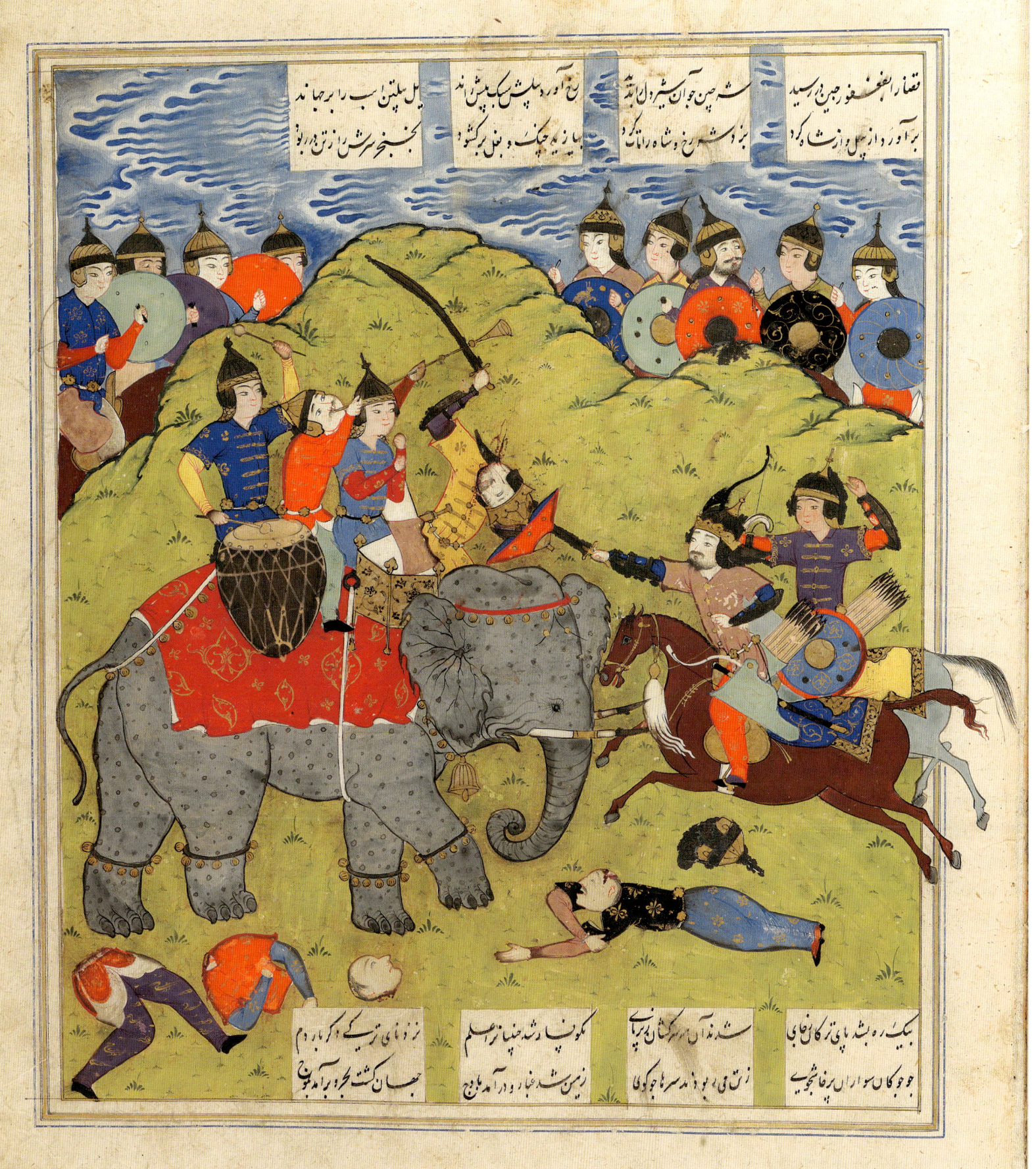

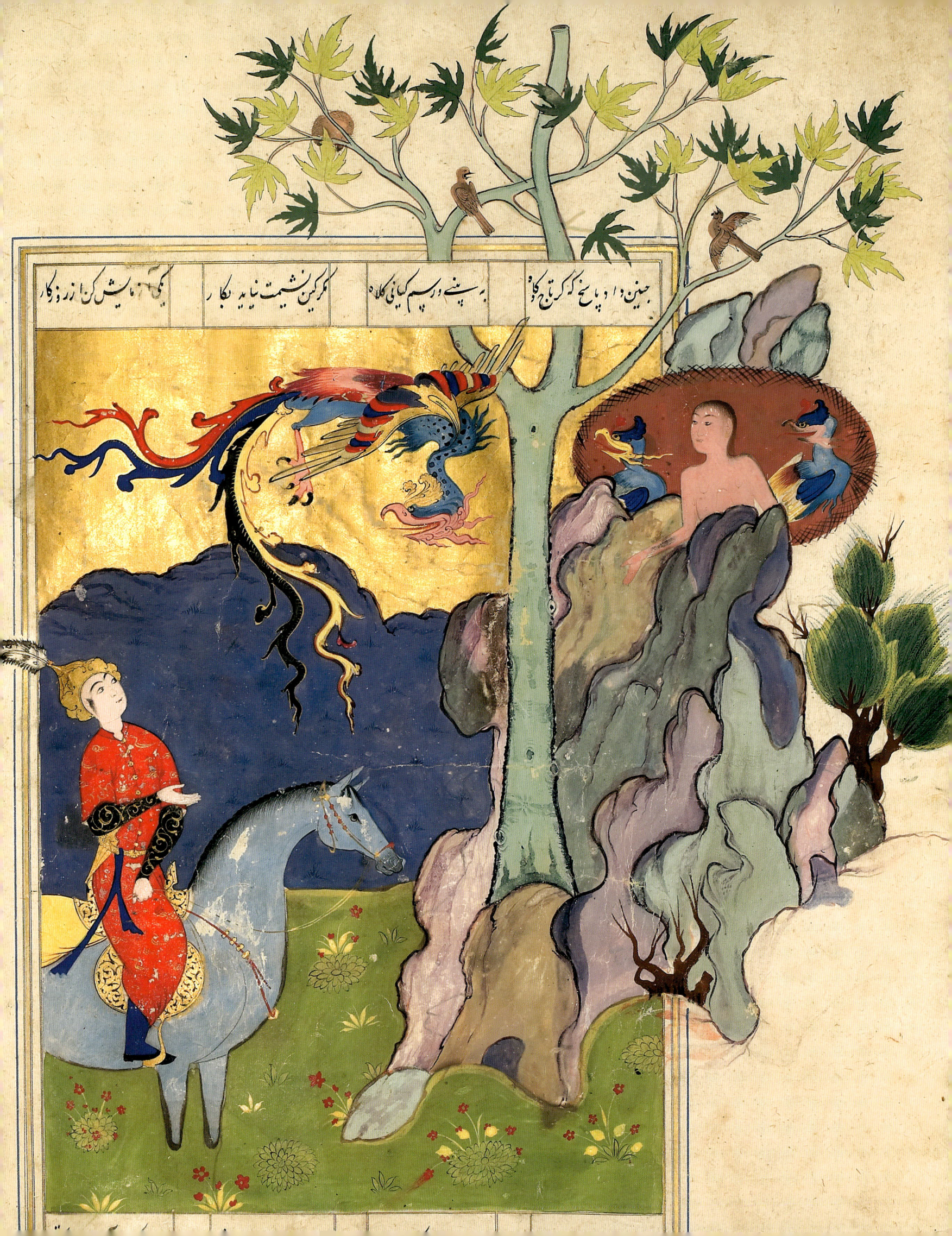

The painting just mentioned (no. 8; illustrated this page) is among the most complex of the manuscript and is clearly the work of many different hands. The fine face of Zal and the organic, delicately painted rocks that spill over the right margin are clearly the work of the 'Ali Asghar-esque artist(s) of the first style. The horse and the grass of the foreground would appear to have been executed by the artist of *Rustam kills Ashkabus*, whom we may consider to have been the least accomplished of the artists who worked on the manuscript, while the finely painted figure of Sam atop the horse is the work of an accomplished artist whose work is not represented elsewhere in the codex.

The Detached Paintings

At some point prior to its sale at Sotheby's in 1935, six folios, all in the 'Ali Asghar-esque style, were detached from the Eckstein *Shahnama*. They reappeared in a 1976 Colnaghi sale, although unfortunately only four of the paintings were illustrated in the accompanying catalogue,[29] in which Basil Robinson classified the paintings as "Qazvin, *c.* 1570" and "perhaps by 'Ali Asghar". Four of the paintings are now in the Nasser D. Khalili Collection and the other two are in private collections. In the list below, these paintings' location in the Eckstein *Shahnama* is given in brackets:

1. *The fire ordeal of Siyavush* (ff. 154–55; fig. 15 on page 58)
Illustrated in Colnaghi's, *Persian and Mughal Art* (London 1976), p. 110. Private collection

2. *Siyavush playing polo before Afrasiyab* (ff. 164–65; fig. 5)
Illustrated *ibid.*, p. 111. Private collection

3. *Kay Khusrau, Farangis and Giw fording the Oxus* (ff. 189–90; fig. 6)
Illustrated *ibid.*, p. 112. Now in the Nasser D. Khalili Collection

4. *Combat of Gushtasp and the dragon* (ff. 377–78; fig. 7)
Now in the Nasser D. Khalili Collection

5. *The dying Rustam shoots Shaghad* (ff. 466–67; fig. 8)
Illustrated *ibid.*, p. 113. Now in the Nasser D. Khalili Collection

6. *Azar Barzin beheading the dragon as it swallows Bahman* (ff. 549–50; fig. 9) Now in the Nasser D. Khalili Collection
Robinson identified the protagonist in this last illustration as Faramurz, though its sequence in the pictorial cycle, coming after the death of the hero, makes this identification impossible. In fact it represents Azar Barzin, the son of Faramurz, who appears in the same scene in the *Bahmannama* section of the 1580 truncated *Shahnama* in All Souls College, Oxford.[30]

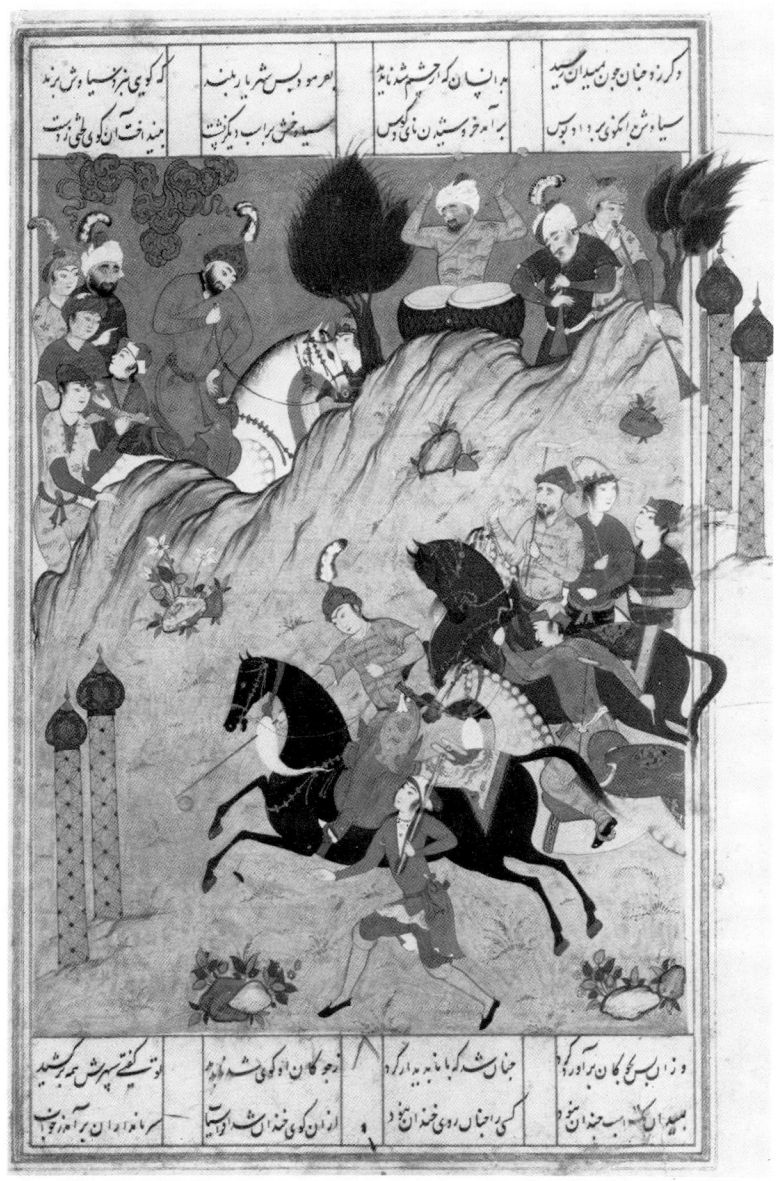

LEFT *Sam asks the Simurgh to return Zal*, no. 8, f. 77v

Zal, son of Sam, one of the heroes of Sistan in eastern Iran, was born with inauspiciously white hair, a feature thought to be demonic. Abandoned on the mountainside as a result, the infant Zal was raised by the miraculous Simurgh, a gigantic but benevolent bird, until the remorseful Sam came to reclaim him. Curiously, it was not uncommon in depictions of Zal to omit the white hair that was the cause of his early misfortune.

ABOVE Fig. 5 *Siyavush playing polo before Afrasiyab*, leaf detached from the Eckstein *Shahnama*, private collection

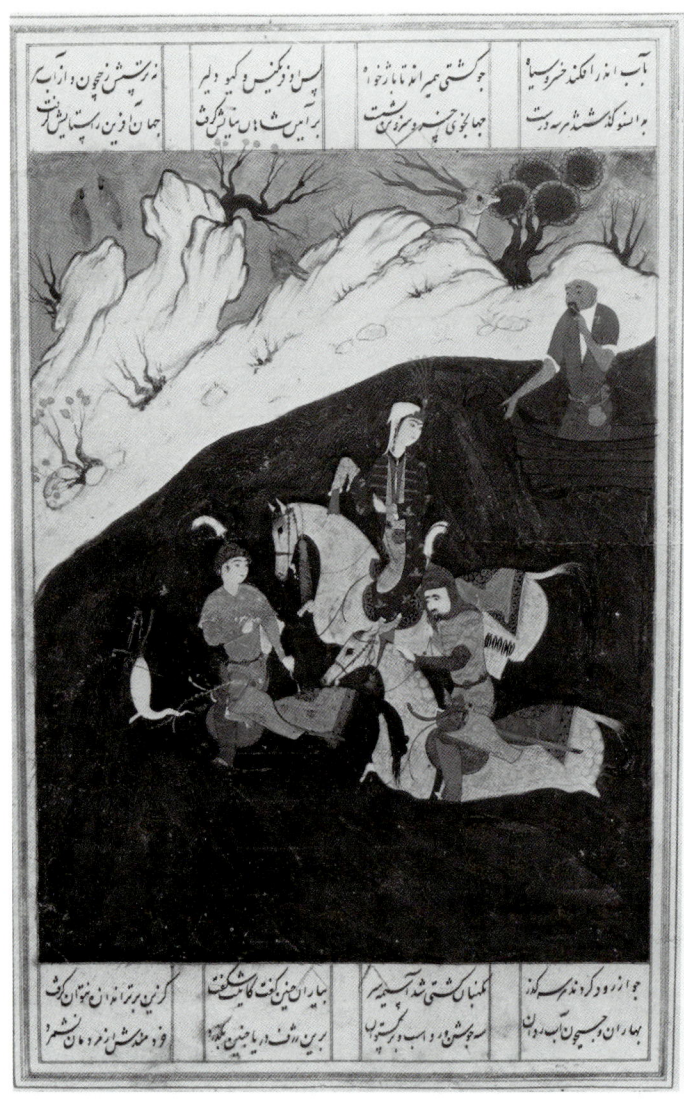

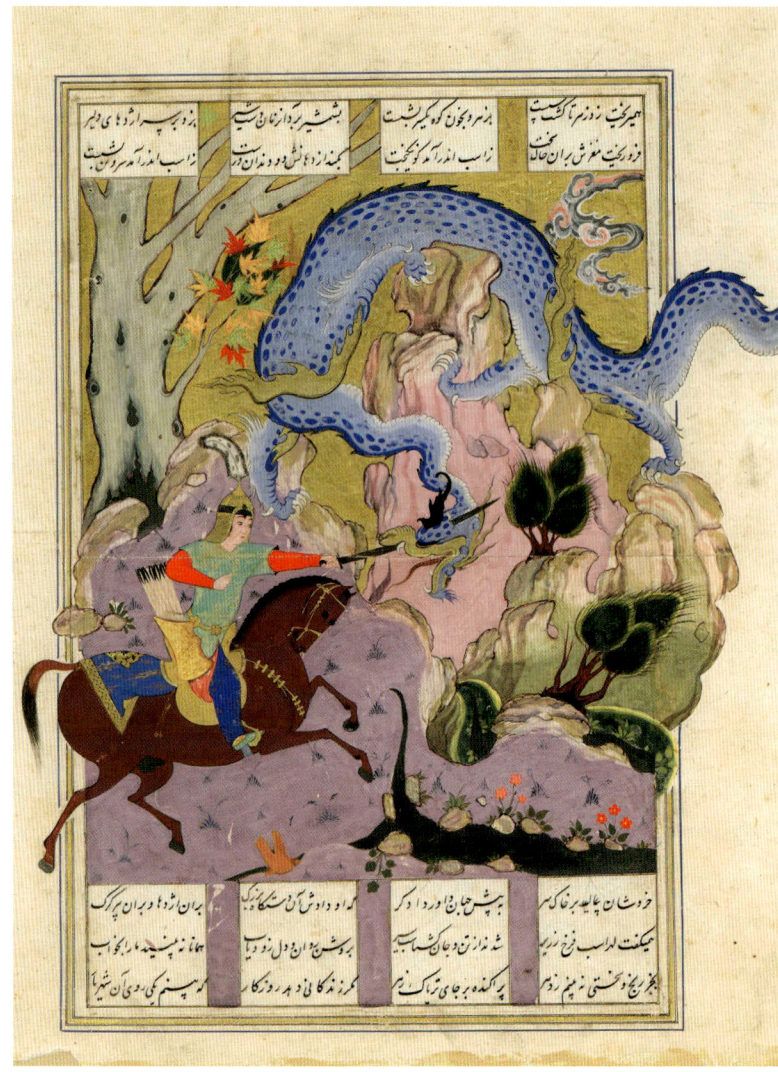

Fig. 6 *Kay Khusrau, Farangis and Giw fording the Oxus*, detached leaf from the Eckstein *Shahnama*, Nasser D. Khalili Collection

Fig. 7 *Combat of Gushtasp and the dragon*, detached leaf from the Eckstein *Shahnama*, Nasser D. Khalili Collection

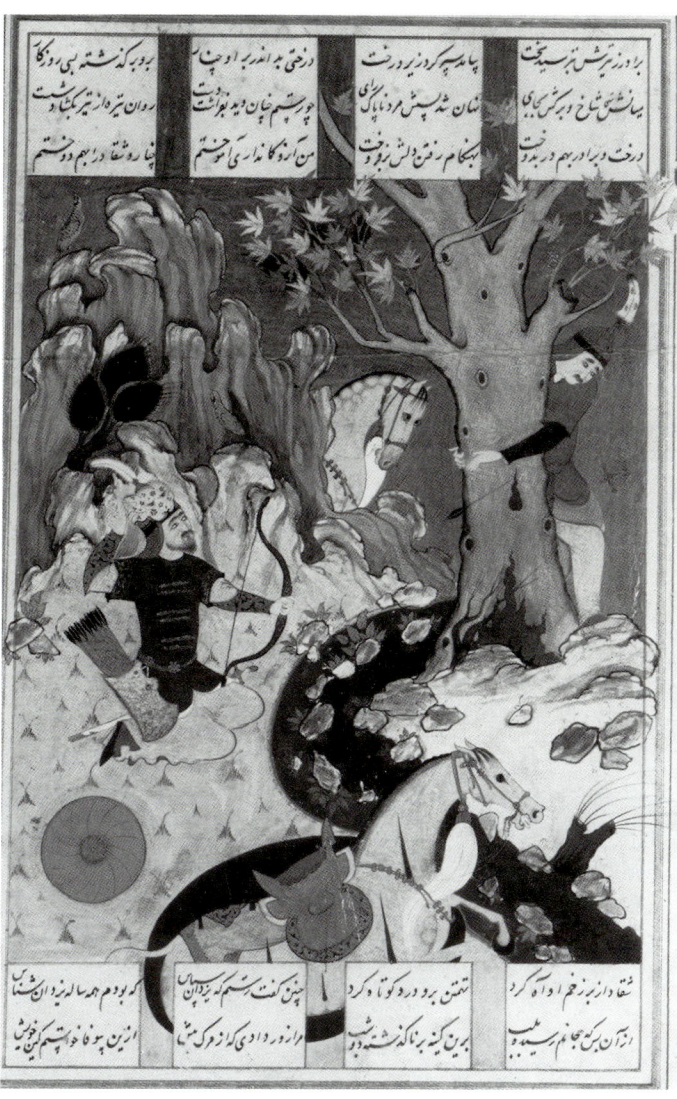

Fig. 8 *The dying Rustam shoots Shaghad*, detached leaf from the Eckstein *Shahnama*, Nasser D. Khalili Collection

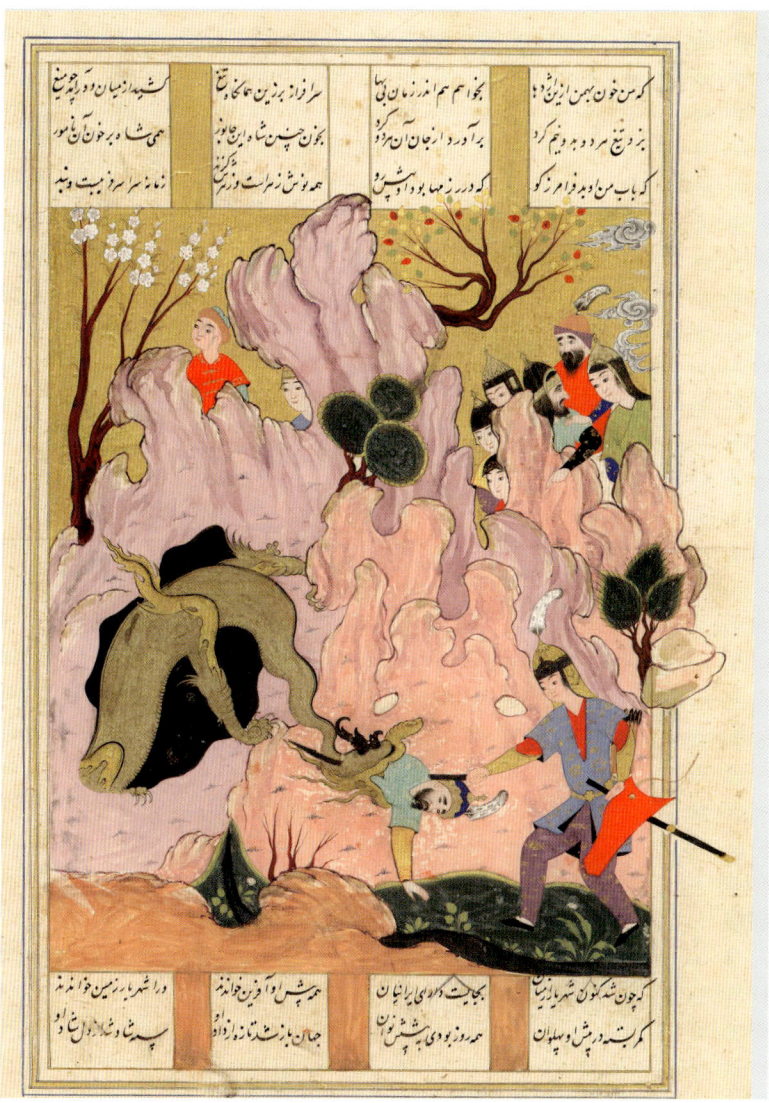

Fig. 9 *Azar Barzin beheading the dragon as it swallows Bahman*, detached leaf from the Eckstein *Shahnama*, Nasser D. Khalili Collection

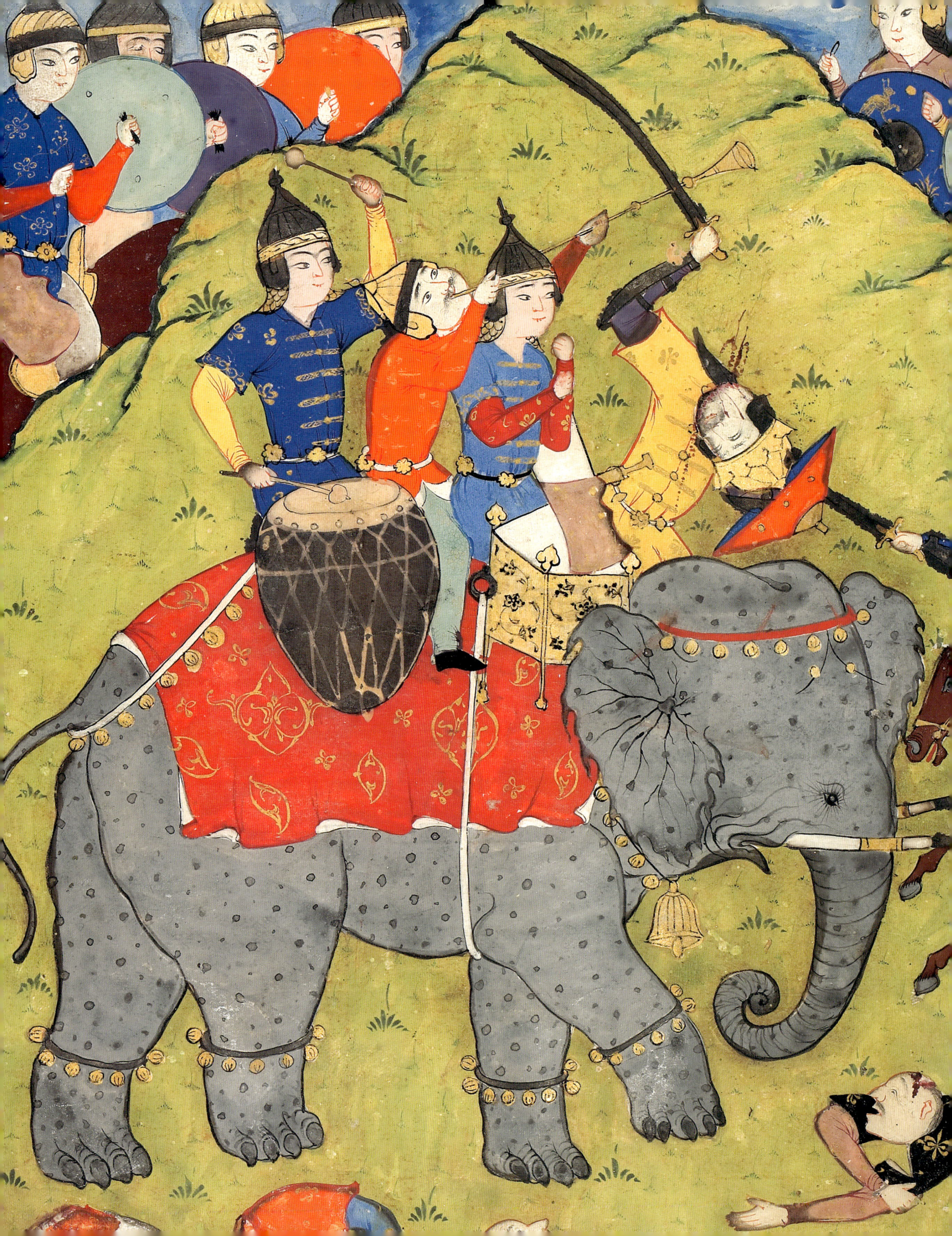

Analysis

The Eckstein *Shahnama* and Ottoman Ideology

Until now the attribution of the truncated *Shahnama* series to the Ottoman Empire has rested on its relation to the *Qisas al-Anbiya'* series. This series, too, however, is remarkably short on colophon information, and in no case is even the place of production stated. There also exists, however, a manuscript of Fuzuli's Turkish mystical romance *Leyla ve Mejnun* executed in the *Qisas* style, in which, as in the Eckstein *Shahnama*, there are one or two indications of an 'Ottomanizing' tendency in some of the miniatures.[31]

Generally speaking, the identification of the *Qisas* series as Ottoman is based on the ideological outlook of the series: the *Qisas al-Anbiya'* manuscripts partake in the Ottoman vision, shared with such works as the *Siyer-i Nebi*, that links the dynastic Ottoman present to the Prophetic past. For the Ottomans, whose claims to legitimacy were at best resourceful, identification with the Prophets created an aura of sanctity around the dynasty at a point in time when religious leadership was increasingly identified with the state.[32]

Establishing the presence of such ideological overtones could prove crucial in securing the attribution of the Eckstein *Shahnama* to the Ottoman Empire. At first sight, the choice of the Iranian national epic as a vehicle for the expression of pro-Ottoman sentiment might seem a strange one, given the hostility that marked Ottoman-Safavid relations throughout the sixteenth century. It would seem particularly strange against the backdrop of the long and bitter Twelve-Year War (1578–90), during the course of which the Eckstein *Shahnama* was produced.

The Ottomans had, however, a long history of involvement with Firdausi's *Shahnama* and the imagery and ideas associated with it. Luxury copies of the manuscript were among the gifts most frequently presented to the sultans by Safavid envoys, the most famous example being the *Shahnama* of Shah Tahmasp, or so-called Houghton *Shahnama*, presented to Sultan Selim II in 1568. Recent research has shown that the Ottomans, besides maintaining the *Shahnama* as a permanent court classic, also experimented with the text and its inherent concepts of kingship and legitimacy. This involved not only the translation of the *Shahnama* into Ottoman Turkish, but also the reworking, in the creation of an Ottoman historical genre, of notions of royal legitimacy found in the *Shahnama*. The post of official court historian, established in 1545, was tellingly

Detail from *Sam kills the Faghfur of Chin*, no. 7, f. 72r

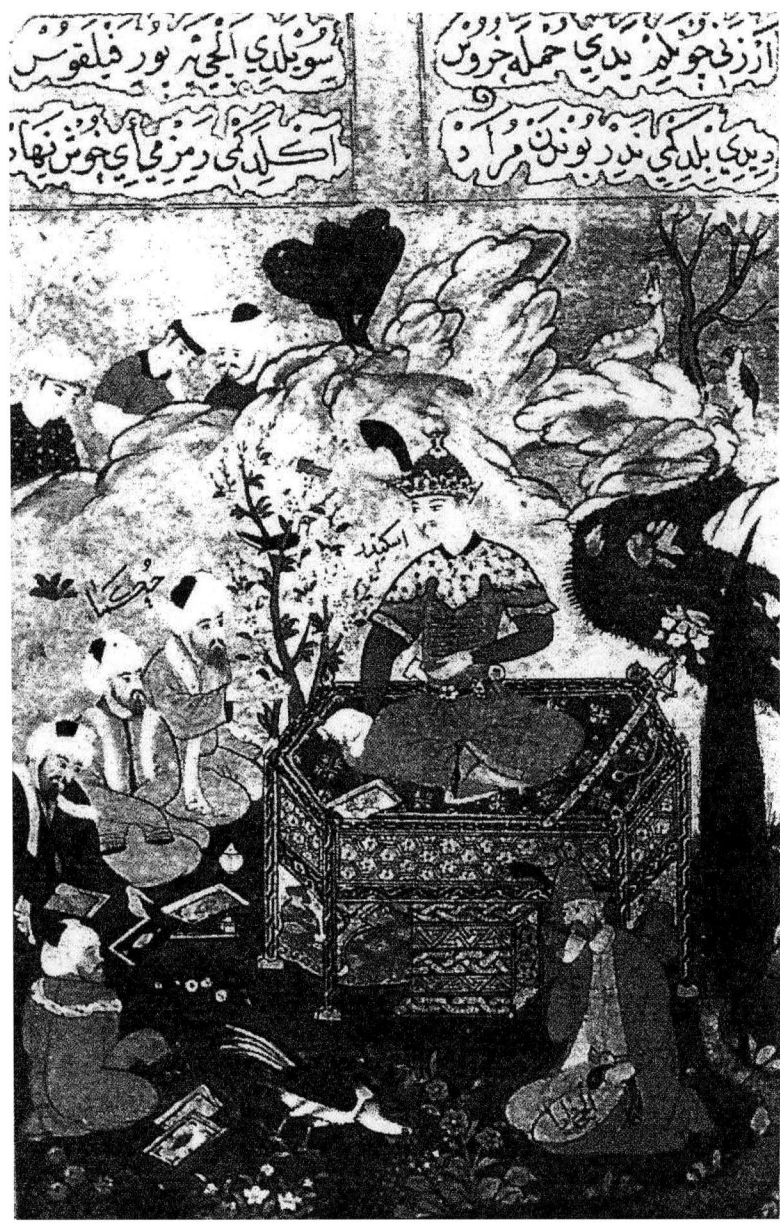

Fig. 10 *Alexander receives the messenger of Dara*, from *Shaja'atnama*, Istanbul University Library, T. 6043, f. 221r

Güner İnal has interpreted this painting as a prediction of the Ottomans' future victory over their Safavid rivals. Veli Can, the probable artist, was a painter trained in the Qazvin court style, active in Istanbul at the time the Eckstein *Shahnama* was produced.

entitled *Şehnameci* (*Shahnama* official), and the histories produced by the holders of this office, such as Aflaki's *Shahnama-yi Al-i 'Uthman* and Seyyid Lokman's *Tarih-i Sultan Süleyman Han*, were classified as *Şehnames*. Though these works were not overtly modelled on the *Shahnama*, it is nonetheless apparent that Ottoman court historians and painters transformed and assimilated the centuries-old textual and visual vocabulary of illustrated *Shahnamas* in depicting the events of the late sixteenth century.[33] The innovation apparent in the truncated *Shahnamas*, and the Eckstein *Shahnama* in particular, with its unusual eleven-part division, would therefore seem consistent with what we know concerning the Ottomans' willingness to experiment with Firdausi's work.

More specifically, the result of reducing the *Shahnama* to its 'mythical' section is to highlight two particular themes. The first of these is the epic struggle to defend the borders of Iran from its foes that dominates the reigns of the kings Kay Ka'us and Kay Khusrau. This conflict must have resonated strongly for readers of the Eckstein *Shahnama*, who were no doubt reminded of the war in which the Ottomans were at that time waging against the Safavids. The traditional association, however, of the Turanians, Iran's major foe in the struggle in the *Shahnama*, with the Turks would seem to make the possibility of any pro-Ottoman bias in the Eckstein *Shahnama* rather unlikely.

The second of the themes highlighted by the truncated *Shahnamas* is Iran's involvement with the Greeks. This begins in earnest with the emigration of Gushtasp to Constantinople in the reign of Luhrasp, and reaches its climax in the reign of Iskandar (Alexander the Great), who in Firdausi's version of events is portrayed as the legitimate ruler of both the Iranians and the Greeks.

An identification of the Ottoman dynasty with Alexander the Great would by no means be without precedent. As far back as the turn of the fifteenth century the poet Ahmedi dedicated to Sultan Süleyman the *İskendername*, a Turkish account in verse of the life of Alexander drawing heavily on the work of Firdausi and Nizami.[34] The identification was made only more explicit after the conquest of Constantinople by Mehmed II in 1453 CE; in the first Ottoman history to be written after this event, the Greek *Historia*, the historian Kritovoulos compares Mehmed II's achievements with those of Alexander.[35] Writing in the reign of Sultan Bayezid, the historian Tursun Bey opens his *History of [Mehmed] the Conqueror* with a Qur'anic verse concerning Dhu'l Qarnayn, frequently identified as Alexander in Ottoman religious scholarship and literature.[36]

Alexander continued to figure large in the Ottomans' eclectic dynastic legitimation and literary imagination. The identification was, of course, a natural one; as *rumi*, a word meaning both 'Greek' and 'Anatolian', the Ottomans portrayed themselves as heirs not only to the Seljuks but also to the Byzantine Empire and the Greek tradition at large. Alexander himself was frequently referred to as *Iskandar-i Rumi* in Persian and Ottoman literature.

In the light of this association, the refocusing of the *Shahnama* around the struggle for Iran and the reign of Alexander the Great in the Eckstein *Shahnama* poses the question whether the truncated *Shahnamas* were not meant to provide, or at least imply the existence of, some sort of justification for the Ottomans' repeated campaigns against Iran's western borders. Though the first dated truncated *Shahnama* predates by five years the outbreak of the Twelve-Year War, nonetheless the coincidence of truncated *Shahnama* production with what must have been a period of mounting hostility might be more than fortuitous.

In presenting an Ottoman version of the Alexander myth in the context of the Ottoman-Safavid conflict the Eckstein *Shahnama* would not stand alone. In an important study of a group of late sixteenth-century Ottoman illustrated manuscripts Güner İnal has furnished us with the example of a *Shaja'atnama* illustrated in Istanbul in 1586 in the Qazvin style, possibly by the painter Veli Can. Veli Can was an artist from Tabriz who figures in Ottoman payrolls of the period and was a former pupil of Siyavush, one of the painters involved in the production of the Shah Isma'il II *Shahnama*. There is more than one connection with the Isma'il II *Shahnama* shared by the *Shaja'atnama* and the Eckstein *Shahnama*. In the same study İnal adduces, as a painting in which the imprint of the Qazvin style is particularly visible, an illustration in the *Shaja'atnama* of Alexander receiving the messenger of Dara, his brother and rival to the throne (fig. 10). In the version of events portrayed by the *Shaja'atnama* Alexander throws some maize on to the ground, which is quickly gobbled up by a cock. İnal has identified a pun behind this curious scene, likening Dara to the maize, *darı* in Turkish, and has interpreted it as a bold statement of the future victory of the Ottoman forces in the war they were currently waging against Iran.[37] This illustration, probably executed in Istanbul by an Iranian artist of the Qazvin court tradition only two years before the completion of the Eckstein *Shahnama*, certainly corroborates the idea that the truncated *Shahnamas* depict a distinctly Ottoman version of Iranian history.

The alternative ending in some of the truncated *Shahnamas* can also be seen to accommodate this thesis. In their scenario, the work finishes not with the reign of Alexander, but with that of Queen Humay. She was a granddaughter of the Greek Emperor, and both daughter and wife to King Bahman. After Bahman's death, in order to keep the throne for herself, Humay cast her son adrift on the Euphrates river in a casket. It was this action that set in motion the unification of Iran and the Greek Empire by Darab, the father of Alexander the Great. Interestingly, in the *Shahnama* it was also the accession of Queen Humay that excluded from the succession the line of Sasan, Humay's half-brother and stepson, which centuries later was to establish the right of the Sasanian dynasty to the throne. Could, then, the reign of Queen Humay be a useful point at which to conclude the *Shahnama*, excising the Sasanians from the pages of Iranian history and anticipating the union of Iran and Rum at the hands of Darab and Alexander?

This anticipated *denouement* might provide the key to an understanding of the unusual format of the manuscript. While both of the endings to the truncated versions of the *Shahnama* are in some sense climactic, neither brings the series of events in the tale to a satisfactory conclusion. The suspense created by the breaking of the narrative invites the reader to seek a conclusion beyond the text in his own time, in which – for the first readers of the Eckstein *Shahnama* – the Ottoman-Safavid war must have loomed large. That the reader was expected to seek a conclusion himself is also suggested by the division, rarely encountered in the Islamic tradition, of the manuscript into eleven chapters. While the number eleven carries no particular significance in the Islamic tradition, the number twelve, however, figures large. The division of the manuscript into eleven chapters would seem to presuppose the existence of a twelfth and final one, which the reader is perhaps invited to locate in his own time, identifying the Ottoman Sultan as the successor to Alexander/Queen Humay and unifier of Rum and Iran.

The number twelve, of course, was of particular significance in the Shi'i tradition, being the number of *imams*, the divinely appointed leaders of the community. It is unlikely that the Ottomans wished explicitly to associate their sultan with the messianic Twelfth Imam of the Shi'i tradition; it might not be so far-fetched, however, to suggest that a twelve-part version of Iranian history, culminating in the unification of Iran and the Ottoman Empire by the Ottoman Sultan, was meant to provide some sort of alternative to the Twelver Shi'i eschatology espoused by the Safavids. While this analysis is far

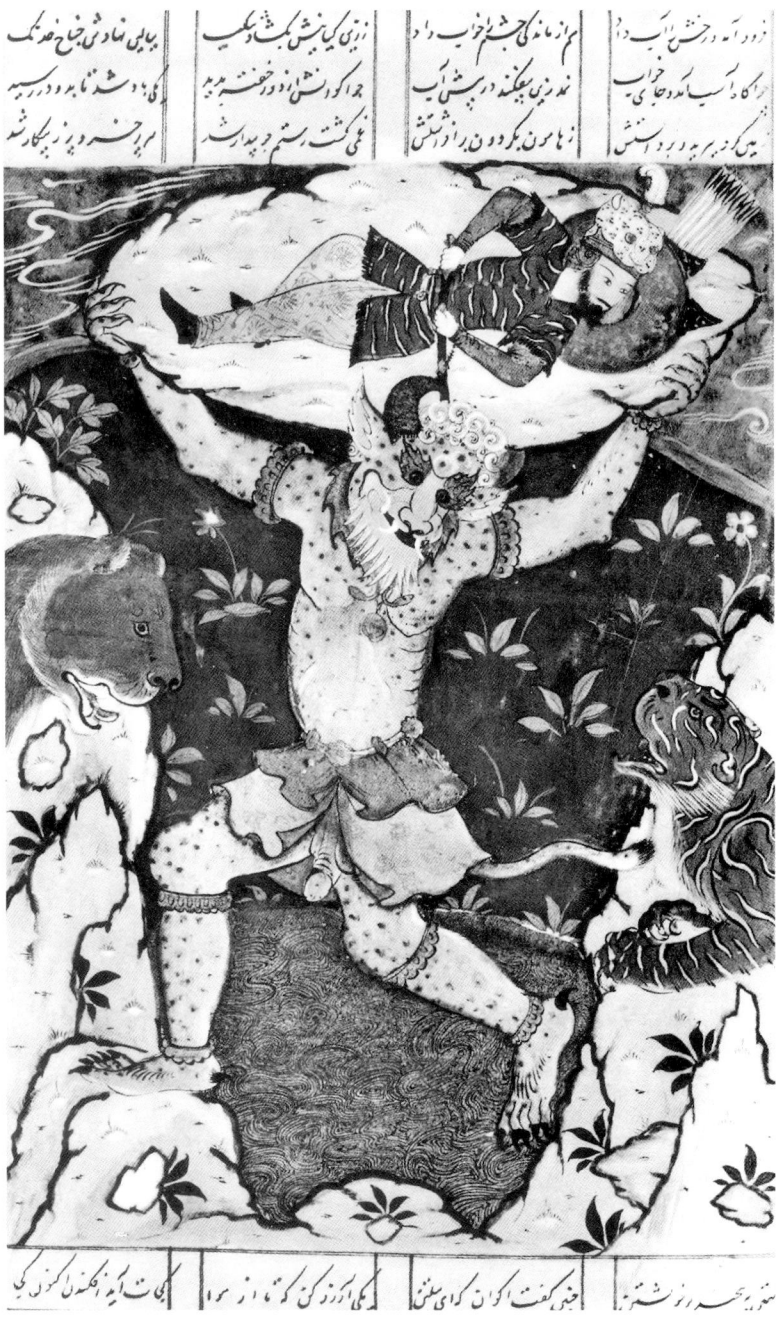

Fig. 11 *Akvan Div flings Rustam into the sea*, from *Shahnama*, Topkapı Saray Müzesi, H. 1487, f. 175

The iconography of this image from another truncated *Shahnama* is derived from the illustration of the same scene in the Eckstein *Shahnama* (no. 18, f. 250v, illustrated page 33) or an earlier Qazvin painting. It appears in a later manuscript (see opposite page) that has been ascribed to Isfahan, but is almost certainly Turkish.

from conclusive, the reworking of an element from Shi'i eschatology would be consistent with the adaptation of Iranian traditions that we have also noted in the painting and illumination of the Eckstein *Shahnama*.

The Eckstein *Shahnama* should not be portrayed, however, as a crude piece of ideology, and it seems unlikely that it or any other of the truncated *Shahnamas* were solely intended to be vehicles for the expression of anti-Safavid sentiment. Their purpose was, above all else, to delight and entertain. If the Eckstein *Shahnama* does indeed make assertions of Ottoman legitimacy, these are insinuated rather than stated. It is also possible that they derive their power from the manuscript's ability to make it appear as if these arose from within the Iranian tradition itself. The lack of colophon information might be connected to this purpose. Though perhaps to be expected in commercial manuscripts, the absence of any mention of patrons or places of production in the truncated *Shahnama* series is conspicuous. Could this in fact be an intended feature of a group of manuscripts that were somehow meant to be authentically Iranian while subtly subverting the Iranian *Shahnama* tradition?

The Eckstein *Shahnama* between Qazvin and the Ottoman Empire

That the painting styles in the Eckstein *Shahnama* are not immediately recognisable as Ottoman may be due to more than a simple desire to appear Iranian. By and large the history of Ottoman painting has been written on the basis of a limited group of court manuscripts, the style of which has come to be defined as quintessentially Ottoman. Certain scholars have, however, for some while now, been aware that a style that appears to be close to Iranian may in fact be Ottoman.[38] The late sixteenth century has been recognised as a period of Iranian influence upon Ottoman painting, a phenomenon frequently attributed to a flow of artists and manuscripts caused by an intriguing combination of intense warfare and heightened commercial exchange with centres of manuscript production such as Shiraz.[39]

The influence of the tradition of Safavid court painting on Ottoman illustrated manuscripts has already been noted in Güner İnal's analysis of the *Shaja'atnama* and other 'Qazvin-influenced' Ottoman manuscripts of the late sixteenth century. In examining the group as a whole İnal notes a tendency over time towards gradual adaptation of features of Qazvini painting to Ottoman tastes, and, in the case of the *Shaja'atname*, a tendency towards a 'less crowded' approach.⁴⁰ Other scholars of Turkish painting, too, have noted the simplification of Iranian styles on their absorption into Ottoman painting.⁴¹ Whether this was a deliberate move in order to accommodate Ottoman tastes is not clear; what we have identified as a self-conscious attempt to make these manuscripts somehow 'Iranian', however, might suggest that it was more a result of a lack of training in Iranian painting and of an inevitable move towards a more Ottoman approach as local artists copied illustrations from other manuscripts.

Various stages of this same process of adaptation and simplification can be identified by comparing the Eckstein *Shahnama* with related manuscripts. It is obvious in the case of *Salm and Tur murder Iraj* in the Eckstein *Shahnama*, which, as we have already noted, bears an iconographic debt to the Isma'il II *Shahnama*. An even greater degree of simplification is seen when we compare the illustration in the Eckstein *Shahnama* of *Akvan Div flings Rustam into the sea* (see page 33) with the same scene in two other manuscripts. The first of these is an undated truncated *Shahnama* in the Topkapı Saray (H. 1487; fig. 11) that apparently belonged to the son of Sinan Pasha.⁴² In this illustration the basic iconography – the demon with his conspicuous genitalia, flanked on either side by a lion and a tiger – is exactly the same as in the illustration from the Eckstein *Shahnama*, though the painting has become simpler and more functional. The large figures are close to the picture plane and set against a simple and symmetrical backdrop outlined with a thick line. The result is strongly reminiscent of the most 'Turkish' paintings in the second style of illustrations in the Eckstein *Shahnama* and presumably represents an advanced stage of the process of adaptation and simplification.

A second version of the scene occurs in a *Shahnama* in the British Library (fig. 12) identified as Isfahani by Basil Robinson, who, however, also noted the puzzling presence of what appear to be four final paintings in the Turkish style, "almost contemporary" with the rest of the paintings.⁴³ Not only the more obviously Turkish miniatures, but also the simplification of the Akvan Div imagery in respect of the Eckstein *Shahnama*, the creamy, glossy paper and the Turkish name of the illuminator in the colophon, 'Çavuşlu', make an Ottoman origin appear now to be more likely.⁴⁴ Even the paintings in what appears to be the Isfahani style of the early seventeenth century have been executed in a reduced, simplified fashion. Should we not conclude from this that Iranian artists and styles continued to influence Ottoman painting into the seventeenth century,

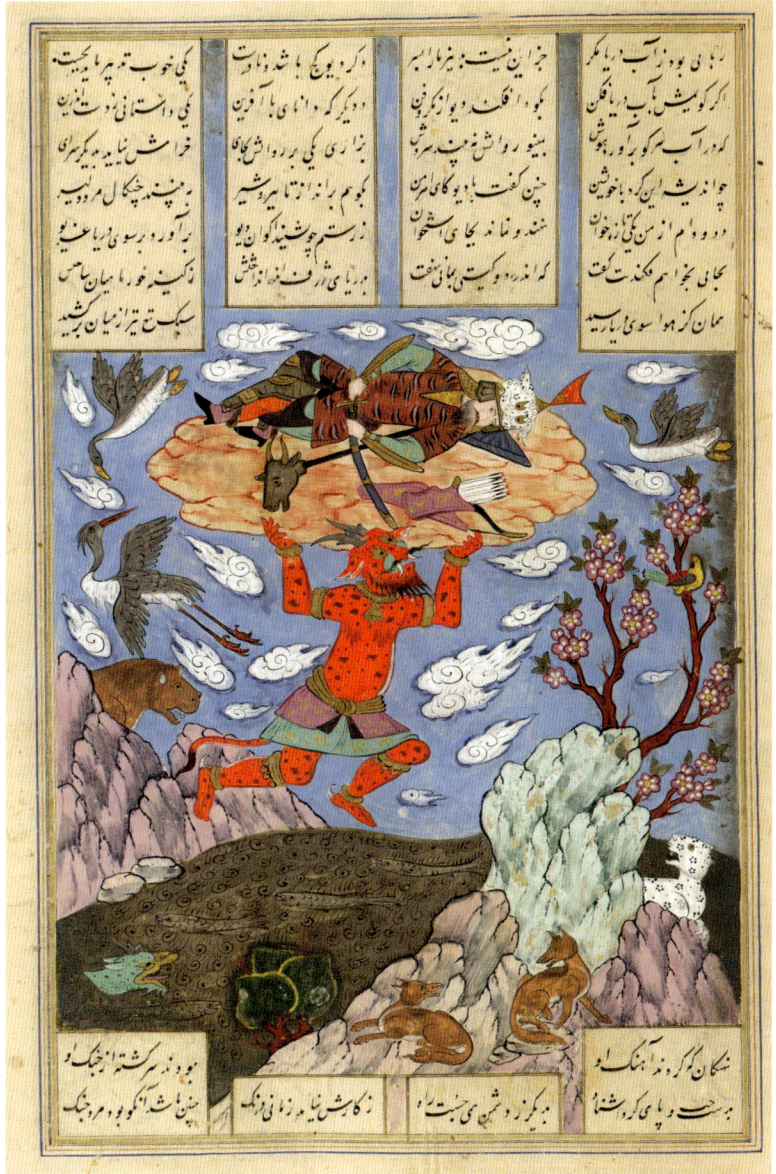

Fig. 12 *Akvan Div flings Rustam into the sea*, from *Shahnama*, British Library, I.O. Islamic 966, f. 189r

This painting is from a *Shahnama* in the British Library previously attributed to Iran, but almost certainly of Turkish origin. The appearance of the iconography used to illustrate the same scene in the Eckstein *Shahnama* (no. 18, f. 250v, illustrated on page 33) is a witness to the continued borrowing by the Ottomans of Iranian styles into the seventeenth century.

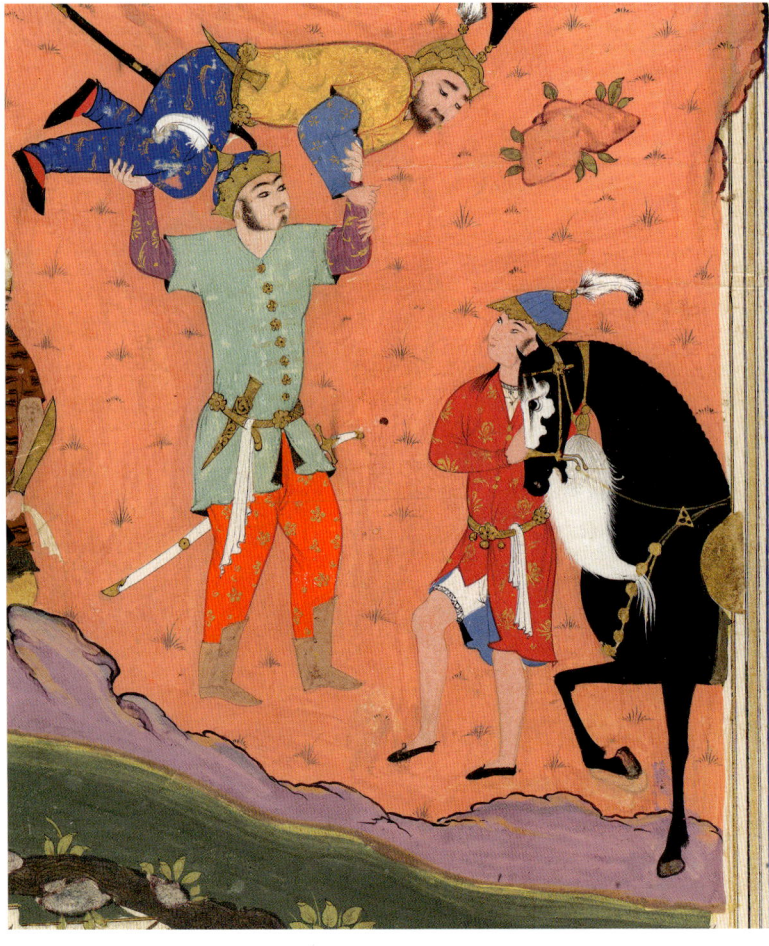

Detail from *Kay Khusrau throws Shida to the ground*, no. 23, f. 340r

particularly in works that dealt with traditionally 'Iranian' topics?

That this was the case is suggested by comparing the 'Ali Asghar-style illustrations in the Eckstein *Shahnama* with the paintings in another truncated *Shahnama* in the Topkapı Saray (H. 1490). This manuscript contains an illustration in the Isfahani style of the early seventeenth century and was therefore produced after the Eckstein *Shahnama*. In the illustration of *Rustam unseating Afrasiyab* (fig. 13) the distinctive profile of the youth in the top left corner and the fine bearded face of Afrasiyab are both clearly derived from the same facial types as in the Eckstein *Shahnama*.[45] Even more conclusive is the depiction of Barzu's mother on horseback, for which the only iconographic precedent is the illustration of the same scene in the Eckstein *Shahnama*.[46] Again, the presence of an illustration in the Isfahani style should lead us to conclude that Iranian styles continued to influence Ottoman illustrations of 'Iranian' works into the seventeenth century.

The identification of this process of the translation of styles should lead us to ask how many illustrations, particularly in the second style, may have ancestors in Iranian and particularly Qazvini painting of the sixteenth century. Certainly, the figure of Manizha in the scene of *Rustam rescuing Bizhan from the pit* (no. 19) strikes one as an adaptation of the Iranian courtly style. Curiously, this illustration is found in almost identical form in two other truncated *Shahnama* manuscripts, one of which is in the Topkapı Saray.[47]

Analysis of the transferral of the imagery and styles of Qazvin painting to Ottoman painting need not be restricted to a study of *Shahnamas* alone. An illustration of *The fire ordeal of Siyavush* (fig. 14) from an undated copy of the *Shahnama* in the Staatsbibliothek zu Berlin, probably from Qazvin, appears to follow a fairly standard model.[48] On one side of the page Siyavush rides into the flames, on the other Kay Ka'us and Sudaba watch the event from the balcony of a flat architectural composition. Of interest to us, however, is the apparently insignificant figure of a man leaning on a stick in a doorway. Interestingly, this figure also appears in the illustration of the same scene that was removed from the Eckstein *Shahnama* (fig. 15).[49] The same figure reappears in the illustration *Nimrod casts Abraham into the fire* in a late sixteenth-century manuscript, almost certainly from Baghdad, of Fuzuli's *Hadiqat al-Su'ada*, along with the fire and the architectural composition (fig. 16).[50] Again, the catapult device used to cast Abraham into the fire in this illustration appears not only in illustrations of the same subject in *Qisas* manuscripts, but also in an *'Aja'ib al-Makhluqat* manuscript that was clearly produced by the ateliers responsible for the *Qisas* and truncated *Shahnama* series.⁵¹ Another link to Baghdad painting stretches back to an early fifteenth-century Baghdad illustration of *Nimrod attempting to fly to Heaven*, the iconography of which was clearly derived from illustrations of *Kay Khusrau in his flying machine* (see page 61).⁵² As *Kay Khusrau in his flying machine* was a popular subject for illustration in truncated *Shahnama*s and depictions of Nimrod using the *Shahnama* iconography were common in Baghdad manuscripts of the 1590s (see, for example, fig. 17), it is possible that the popularity of the former affected the latter.⁵³

Clearly, then, the *Qisas* and *Shahnama* ateliers shared with Baghdad painters a common stock of imagery that they adapted to suit a variety of subjects. The precise relationship between the manuscripts in question, however, is unclear, and the likelihood of direct borrowing of iconography from one by another is unlikely. A more probable explanation is that certain elements in all the manuscripts share a common Qazvini ancestry and found their way into Turkish painting in the second half of the sixteenth century through the migration of artists or the movement of manuscripts. Perhaps the most interesting question is whether borrowings from one genre to another were purely accidental, or were deemed particularly appropriate for certain subjects. It is also worth noting that the transfer of imagery also took place within Ottoman genres, such as the *Qisas al-Anbiya'* and the truncated *Shahnama* series. Rührdanz has already noted the incorrect depiction of Bahman being swallowed headfirst by a dragon in some of the truncated *Shahnama*s, in opposition to the text of the *Bahmannama*, which specifies the correct direction as from the feet up. This error was almost certainly caused by the direct transfer of the imagery used in the *Qisas* series for the depiction of *Musa's rod swallowing the magicians of Egypt*.⁵⁴ In connection with the Eckstein *Shahnama*, we might note the presence of the angel Surush half concealed by the rocks in the left corner in the illustration *Faridun brings Zahhak to Mount Damavand* (no. 3; see page 62). Though Surush is mentioned just before this event in Firdausi's text, his inclusion in this illustration appears to be unprecedented, though he appears again in a later Ottoman *Shahnama* (see fig. 18), dated to *c*. 1630 by Stchoukine.⁵⁵ This, of course, raises the possibility that his inclusion in the Eckstein *Shahnama* was due to the influence of Ottoman copies of the *Qisas al-Anbiya'*, or the *Siyer-i Nebi*, in which such elongated angels proliferate.

A full analysis of the ways in which the Ottomans used the vocabulary of Persian painting and transferred the imagery of one genre to another lies outside the scope of this publication. It is

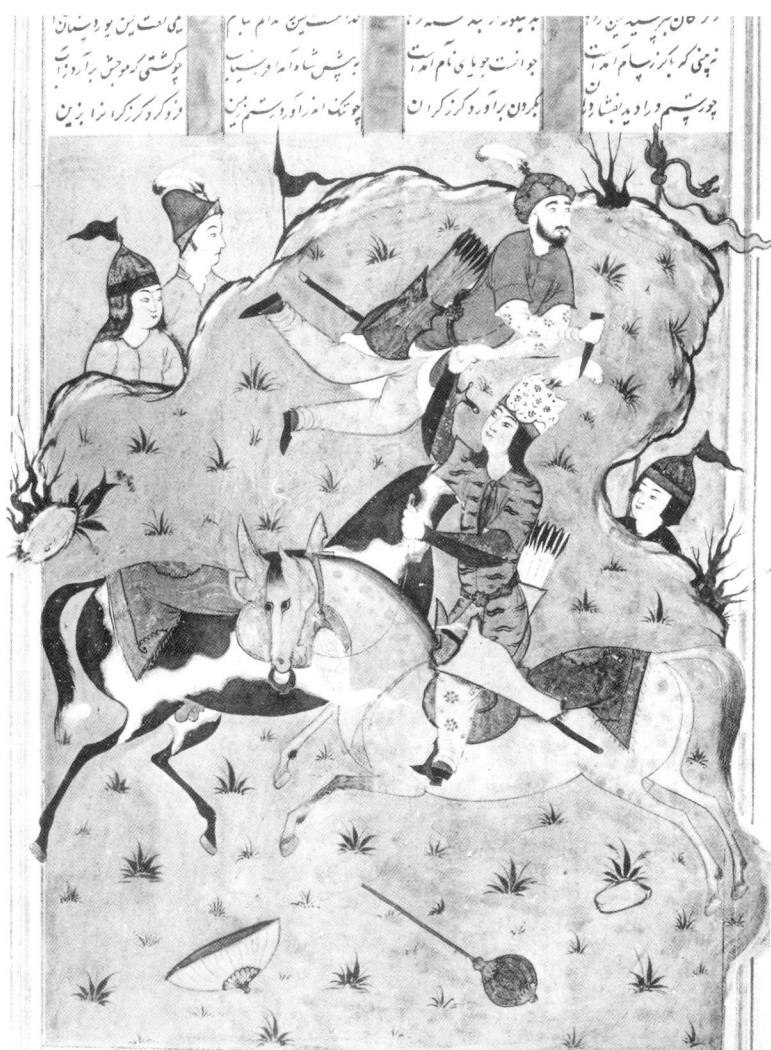

fig. 13 *Rustam unseating Afrasiyab*, from *Shahnama*, Topkapı Saray Müzesi, H. 1490, f. 25v

Afrasiyab's face with its pointed beard and the face of the figure in profile are similar to many of the "Ali Asghar-esque' facial types found in the Eckstein *Shahnama* (for example, *Kay Khusrau throws Shida to the ground*, f. 340r, detail illustrated opposite), and may be the result of its influence.

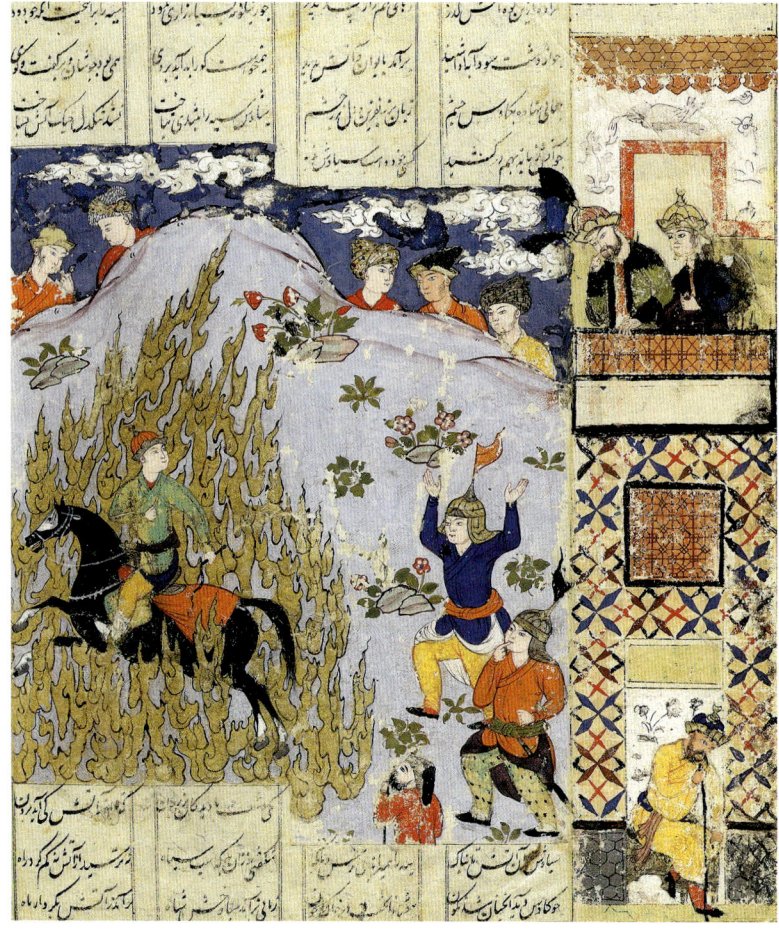 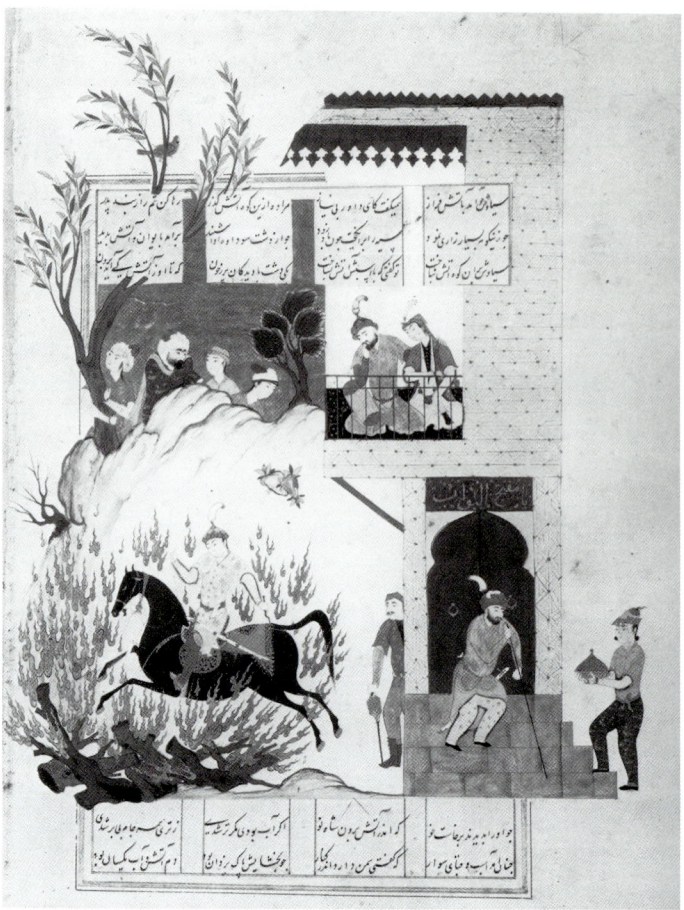

Fig. 14 *The fire ordeal of Siyavush*, from *Shahnama*, Staatsbibliothek zu Berlin, Preussicher Kulturbesitz, Berlin, Orientabteilung, Diez A fol. 1, f. 142v

The iconography of this 1590s painting, probably from Qazvin, is close to that of the illustration of the same scene from the Eckstein *Shahnama*, now in a private collection (see right). In Baghdad painting the same iconography was borrowed for illustrating different subjects, as in *Nimrod casts Abraham into the fire* in a manuscript now in the Los Angeles County Museum (see illustration on opposite page).

Fig. 15 *The fire ordeal of Siyavush*, detached leaf from the Eckstein *Shahnama*, private collection

worth noting, however, that the question of the relationship between kingship and prophecy was one that was of particular concern to the Ottomans, and that where the transfer of iconography has taken place it has generally been between works that deal with one or other of these issues. The career of an Ottoman poet and historian like Uzun Firdevsi ('Long Firdausi') serves to illustrate how interest in these topics could coincide. Famous as the author of the *Süleymanname*, a vast encyclopaedia that had at its core a compilation of all the traditions relating to the prophet Solomon, he penned a Turkish translation of the *Shahnama* as well as a Turkish *İskendername*.[56] Though Uzun Firdevsi died probably more than half a century before the Eckstein *Shahnama* was completed, the convergence of the same themes of prophecy, kingship and the *Shahnama* and Alexander traditions in his literary output may suggest that the sharing of iconography between the truncated *Shahnama*s and other Persian and Ottoman manuscripts had an ideological basis to some degree.

Conclusion

The two major centres for production of illustrated manuscripts in the Ottoman Empire in the late sixteenth century were Istanbul and Baghdad. Baghdad has been proposed as the origin of one of the truncated *Shahnama* manuscripts on the basis of certain stylistic similarities with paintings from the Baghdad school of the 1590s. Scholars have long been aware of the influence of Qazvin painting on the Baghdad school, and that there was a link between Baghdad and Western Iranian painting we have already seen – in the use of imagery from *The fire ordeal of Siyavush* in the *Hadiqat al-Su'ada*. In another *Hadiqat al-Su'ada* manuscript in the Bibliothèque nationale we can again observe similar conical necks, round heads and high turbans, rendered in a simplified style that bears some resemblance to paintings in the second style in the Eckstein *Shahnama*.[57]

The similarities between Baghdad painting and the present manuscript are, however, slight, and might be easily explained by common origins in Qazvin painting rather than by the direct influence of artists or manuscripts. Furthermore, there is no documented school of painting in Baghdad for the 1580s, and even if one were to argue for the existence of one on the basis of the Eckstein and other truncated *Shahnama*s, one would expect a much greater crossover with the Baghdad school of the 1590s in terms of style and iconography than is the case. Whereas Baghdad figures are characteristically small and squat, in the Eckstein *Shahnama* there is a

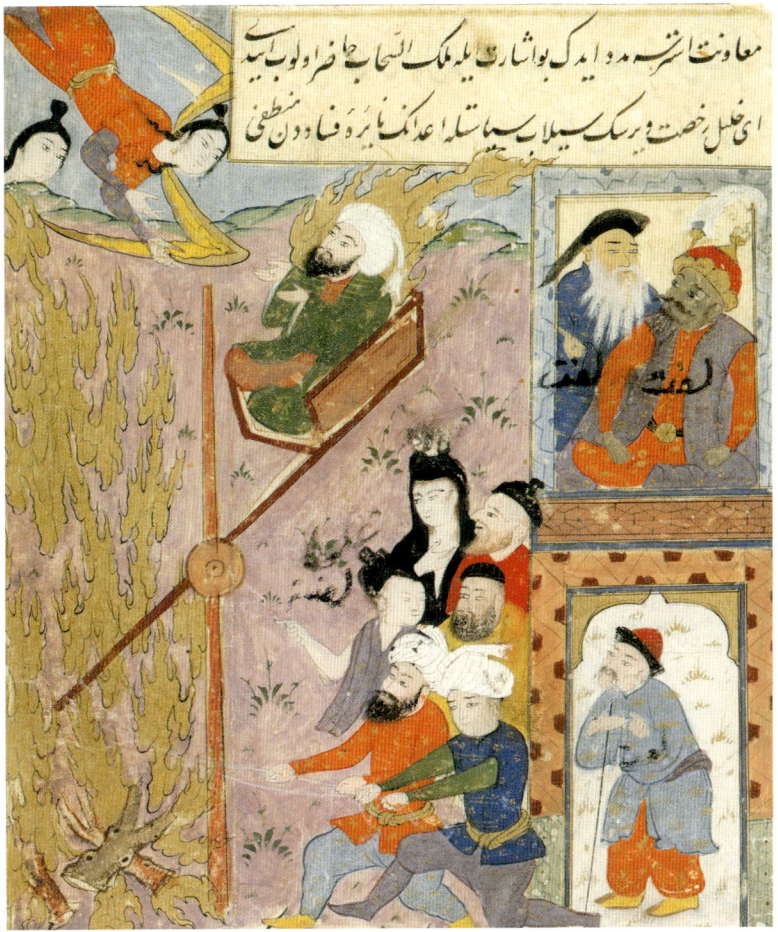

Fig. 16 *Nimrod casts Abraham into the fire*, from *Hadiqat al-Su'ada*, Los Angeles County Museum, M. 85.237, formerly in the collection of Edwin Binney, 3rd (no. 32b)

This illustration from a Baghdad manuscript of the 1590s derives its iconography from illustrations of *The fire ordeal of Siyavush* found in *Shahnama* manuscripts in the Qazvin style (see illustration on opposite page).

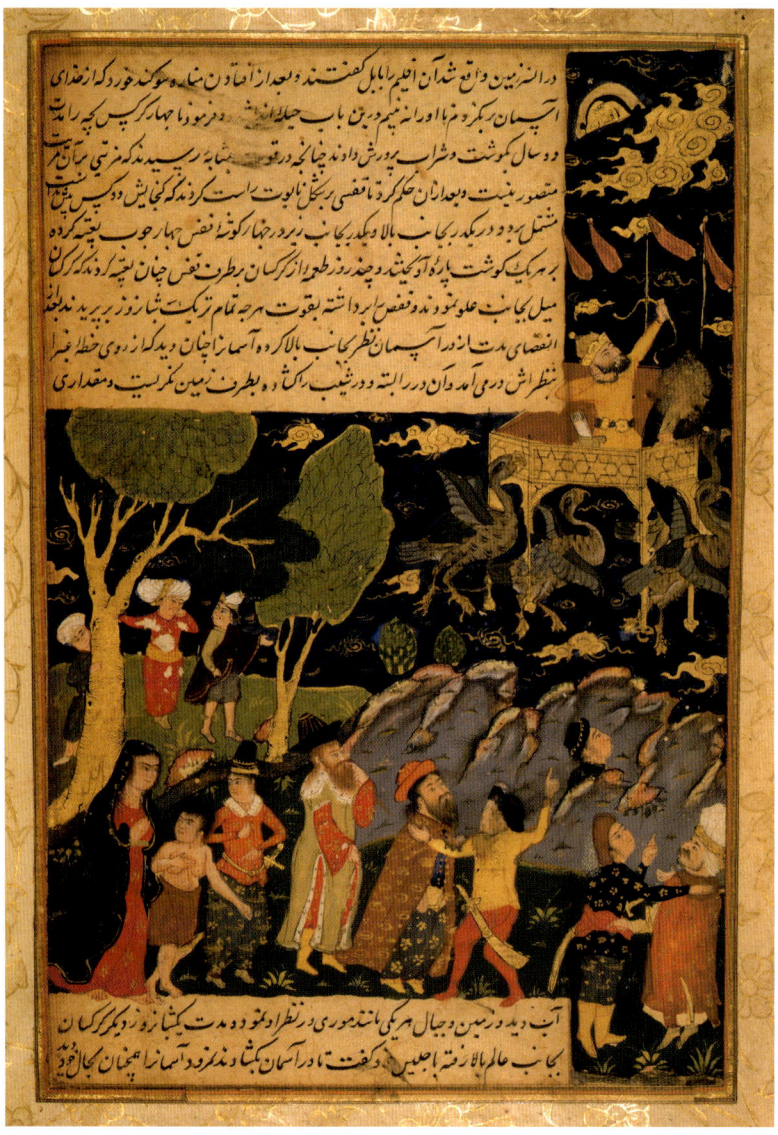

ABOVE Fig. 17 *Nimrod casts Abraham into the fire*, from *Rawdat al-Safa'*, Israel Museum, Jerusalem, inv. 539.69

Illustrations of this scene clearly derived their iconography from depictions of *Kay Khusrau in his flying machine* in *Shahnama* manuscripts. Illustrations of both Nimrod and Kay Khusrau seem to have been popular in late sixteenth-century Ottoman painting.

RIGHT *Kay Ka'us in his flying machine*, no. 12, f. 129v

Kay Ka'us was persuaded by Iblis, the Devil, to find a means of establishing his dominion over the skies as well as the earth. Kay Ka'us's solution was to tie pieces of meat on each corner of his throne and secure eagles just below them. Though the eagles' initial efforts to reach the meat succeeded in lifting the throne aloft, they soon tired, and Kay Ka'us had to be rescued once more by the tireless Rustam.

clear progression towards a larger figural type. In addition, the Baghdad manuscripts are relatively small, the height of the page rarely exceeding 28 cm. In Istanbul manuscripts of the 1580s, however, there is a distinct tendency towards the grandiose: a copy of the *Zübdetü't-Tevarih* dated 1583 measures an impressive 65 x 42 cm, while a *Hünername* completed in 1584/85 and measuring 49 x 31 cm is only slightly taller than the Eckstein *Shahnama* in its present trimmed state.[58] Furthermore, the outstanding illumination, fine paper and cosmopolitan mixture of styles seem more redolent of Istanbul production than of the earthy realism of Baghdad, the output from which appears remarkably homogeneous. Certainly we can imagine, too, that the Eckstein *Shahnama*'s ideological overtones and its incorporation of self-consciously Iranian styles would have resonated strongly in the imperial capital.

The attribution here of the Eckstein *Shahnama* to the Ottoman Empire takes account of the fact that a growing body of illustrated manuscripts which were once thought to be Persian have more recently been attributed to the Ottoman Empire. This 'rediscovery' of a whole corpus of Ottoman paintings should lead to a re-evaluation of the characteristics that art historians look upon as particularly 'Ottoman'. Certain features that the Eckstein *Shahnama* shares with other manuscripts recently identified as Ottoman may be useful for identifying Ottoman manuscripts in the future. In addition to the creamy paper and the fine but idiosyncratic illumination, these include the diversity of painting styles and a tendency to borrow Iranian styles while simplifying them in the process.

Attributions based purely on stylistic criteria, however, will inevitably be complicated by the very fluidity of artists and ideas between Iran and the Ottoman Empire in the late sixteenth and early seventeenth century that this study has sought to elucidate. It is at this stage that an inquiry into the historical context of Ottoman painting and the attempt to identify an Ottoman 'ethos' may prove rewarding. The Ottomans were remarkable for portraying themselves as the heirs, in the strict sense of the word, to diverse cultural and historical traditions.[59] It is precisely this fondness for self-portrayal as the culmination of various historical and eschatological processes that gives so much of Ottoman cultural production a distinctly experimental feel. The Eckstein *Shahnama*, it seems, shares this ethos, and may constitute evidence that the Ottomans sought to reorganize and put their seal on yet another literary-historical tradition. While unravelling the often subtle Ottoman ethos that may inform a manuscript is, of course, the area of research most fraught with conjecture, it may also be potentially the most rewarding.

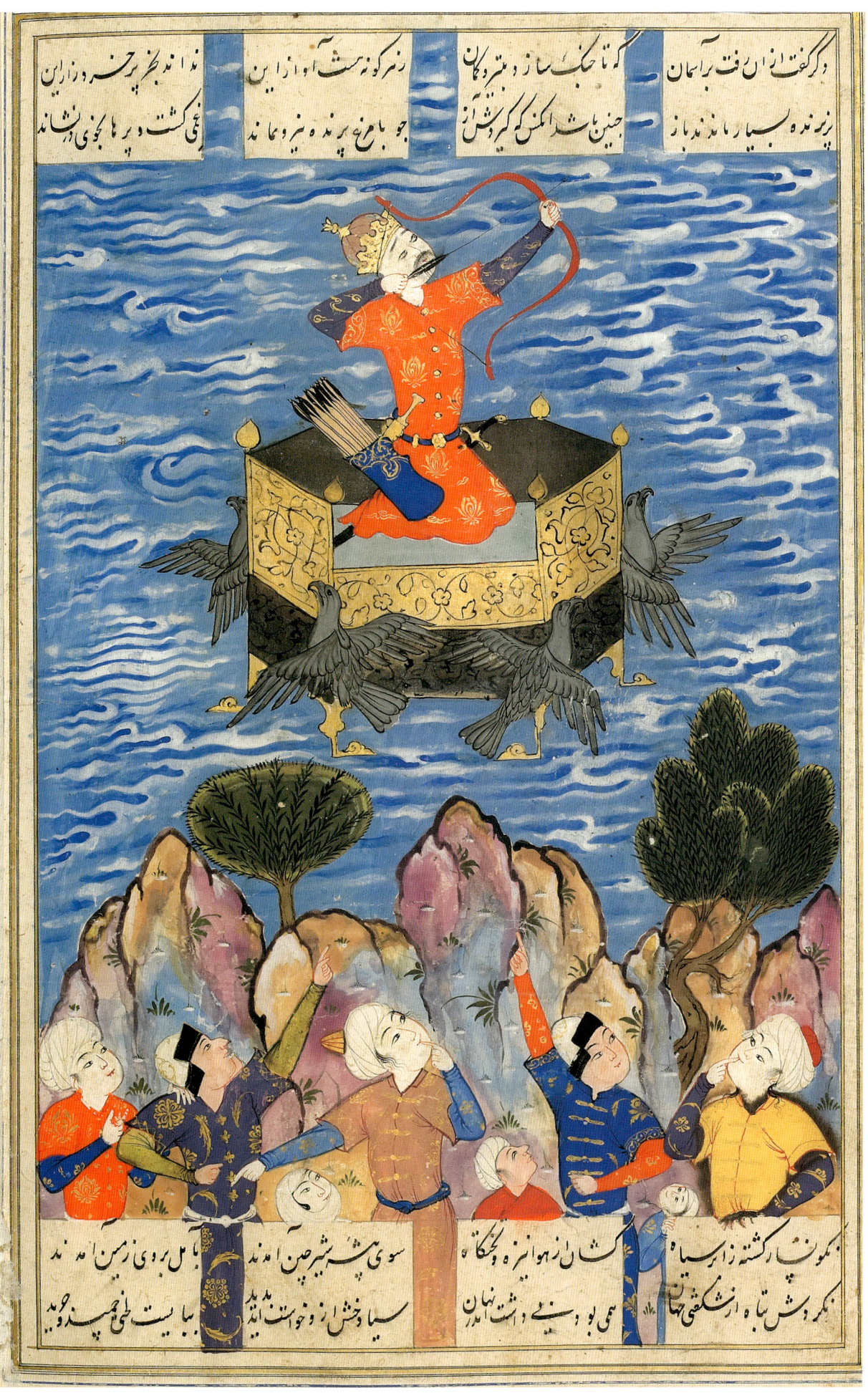

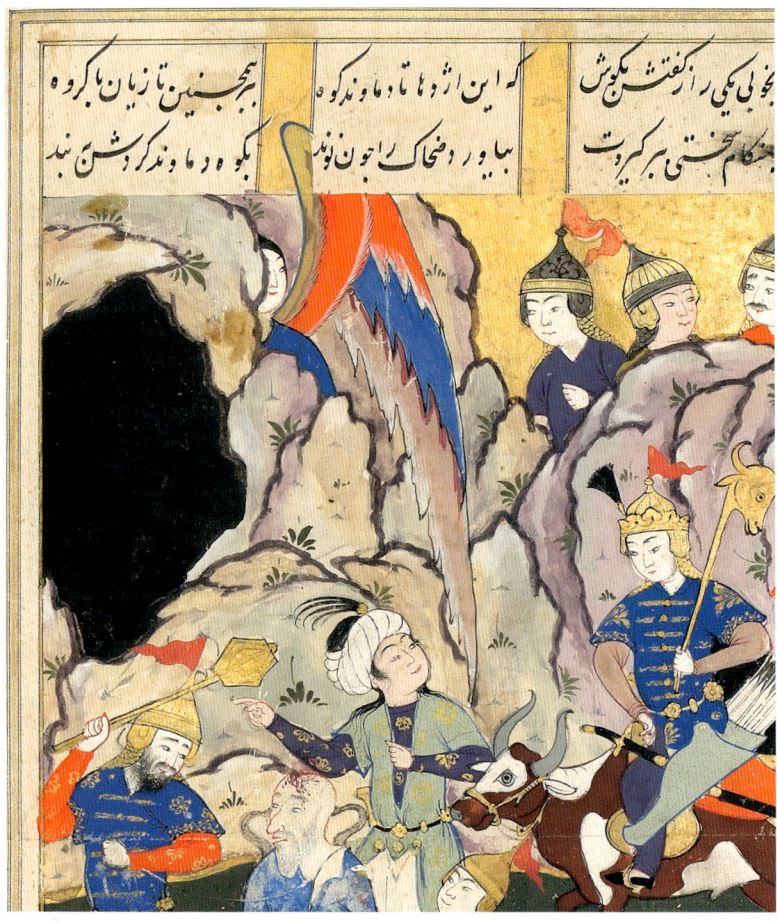

LEFT ABOVE Detail from *Faridun brings Zahhak to Mount Damavand*, no. 3, f. 22v

Zahhak, the evil king of Arabia, established a tyranny over Iran. On his shoulders were two snakes, growing where the despot had been kissed by the Devil. In order to lessen the pain that these snakes caused him, Zahhak fed them on two youths daily. Zahhak's tyranny lasted until he was chained above a chasm on Mount Damavand by the future king Faridun. In the background is the angel Surush, who was responsible for devising the manner of Zahhak's punishment. It is unusual for Surush to be depicted in illustrations of the scene, and his presence here may be due to the influence of the *Qisas al-Anbiya'* series or other Ottoman religious paintings, in which such angels proliferated.

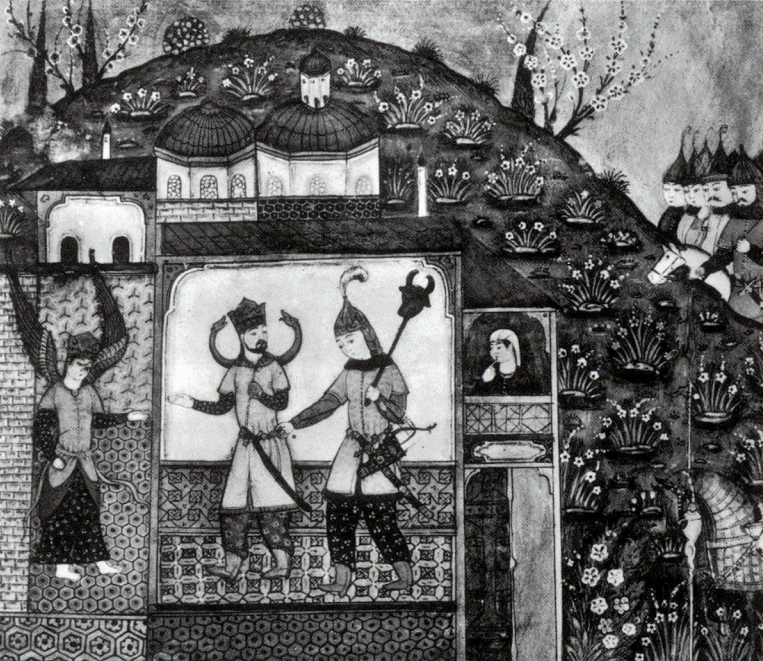

LEFT BELOW Fig. 18 *Faridun brings Zahhak from Mount Damavand*, from *Shahnama*, Topkapı Saray Müzesi, H. 1116, f. 14v

Though his presence is licensed by Firdausi's text, it was rare for illustrations of this scene to depict the angel Surush. The angel appears in the illustration of this scene in the Eckstein *Shahnama*, probably as a result of the influence on *Qisas al-Anbiya'* manuscripts, in which such figures proliferate. As this illustration of the same scene from a later *Shahnama* shows, some Ottoman copies of the *Shahnama* followed the precedent set by the Eckstein *Shahnama*.

NOTES

1 See Oleg Grabar and Sheila Blair, *Epic Images and Contemporary History: The Illustrations of the Great Mongol Shahnama* (Chicago 1980).
2 Karin Rührdanz, "About a Group of Truncated *Shahnamas*: A Case Study in the Commercial Production of Illustrated Manuscripts in the Second Part of the Sixteenth Century", *Muqarnas*, 14 (1997), pp. 118–34.
3 I am grateful to Helen Loveday for shedding light on this little-studied aspect of Ottoman book production.
4 Colnaghi's, *Persian and Mughal Art* (London 1976), pp. 31–32.
5 I am grateful to Manijeh Bayani for this identification.
6 I am grateful to Nabil Saidi for this attribution.
7 Sotheby's, London, 5 February 1935, lot 15.
8 Sotheby's, London, 7 February 1949, lot 1; see also Sotheby's, *Catalogue of Important Oriental Manuscripts and Miniatures: The Property of the Hagop Kevorkian Fund*, 7 April 1975, lot 190.
9 Rührdanz 1997, esp. pp. 129–30.
10 Mirza Muhammad Qazvini, 'Muqaddima-yi qadim-i *Shahnama*', in *Hazara-yi Firdausi* (Tehran 1322/1944), pp. 151–76.
11 I am grateful to Karin Rührdanz for this last observation. Discussions with Dr Rührdanz have been invaluable in constructing many of the arguments found here.
12 No full study has been conducted on the topic of distinguishing scribal error from mistakes made due to unfamiliarity with Persian. The correlation between number of errors and attention paid to illustration and illumination has been noted, however, in L.T. Giuzalian and M.M. Diakonov, *Rukopisi Shah-name v Leningradskih Sobraniiah* (Leningrad 1934).
13 I am grateful to Eleanor Sims for bringing this feature to my attention.
14 Topkapı Saray Müzesi, TKS EH. 227, ff. 1b-2a. For an illustration and the attribution of the illumination to the Safavids see J.M. Rogers and R.M. Ward, *Süleyman the Magnificent* (London 1988), pp. 72–73.
15 Freer Gallery of Art, inv. 46.12, ff. 110v, 253r; illustrated in Marianna Shreve Simpson, *Sultan Ibrahim Mirza's 'Haft Awrang'* (Washington, D.C. 1997), pp. 131, 198.

16 Rührdanz 1997, pp. 125–26.
17 See Rachel Milstein, Karin Rührdanz, Barbara Schmitz, *Stories of the Prophets* (Costa Mesa 1999), chap. 3, 'The Painting Styles of the *Qisas al-Anbiya*' Manuscripts', pp. 41–63.
18 Colnaghi's 1976, pp. 31–32. For a more detailed argument for this attribution see B.W. Robinson, "Ali Asghar, Court Painter', *Iran*, 26 (1988).
19 Rührdanz 1997, p. 120.
20 See Rührdanz's analysis of the 'first style' in Milstein *et al.* 1999, pp. 43–46.
21 Sheila Canby notes the disappearance of 'Ali Asghar from the records in Sheila R. Canby, *The Golden Age of Persian Art, 1501–1722* (London 1999), pp. 88–89.
22 Berlin, Staatsbibliothek zu Berlin, Preussicher Kulturbesitz, Orientabteilung, Diez A fol. 3, f. 50v; illustrated in Milstein *et al.* 1999, pl. II, p. 250.
23 See Rührdanz's discussion of the 'second style' *ibid.*, pp. 46–48.
24 As Rührdanz notes in Milstein *et al.* 1999, p. 48, Stchoukine was the first scholar to attribute paintings in this style to the Ottoman Empire, with reference to TSM. H. 1487 and TSM H. 2149, the two truncated *Shahnamas* in the Topkapı Saray Müzesi mentioned below; see Ivan Stchoukine, *La Peinture Turque, IIème Partie* (Paris 1971), pp. 62–63.
25 Dublin, Chester Beatty Library, Per. 256 03.
26 For the life of this artist see Anthony Welch, *Artists for the Shah* (New Haven and London 1976), p. 212.
27 Bibliothèque nationale, Persan 54. For paintings from this manuscript see Francis Richard, *Splendeurs Persanes* (Paris 1997), p. 122, and Milstein *et al.* 1999, pls. XXI, XXII.
28 Oxford, Codrington Library, All Souls College, ms. 288. A single illustration from this manuscript is illustrated in Rührdanz, p. 121, fig. 3.
29 See note 4.
30 Oxford, Codrington Library, All Souls College, ms. 288, f. 33a; for illustration see Welch 1976.
31 For some of the 'Ottomanizing' tendencies in the *Qisas* series, particularly in the second style, and for the copy of Fuzuli's *Leyla ve Mecnun*, see Milstein *et al.* 1999, pp. 48–51.
32 See *ibid.*, pp. 32–38.
33 See Christine Woodhead, 'An experiment in official historiography: the post of Şehnameci in the Ottoman empire, c. 1555–1605', *Wiener Zeitschrift für die Kunde des Morgenlandes*, 75 (1983), pp. 157–82; F. Sinem Eryilmaz, 'The Official Ottoman Shehname: An Instance of Cultural Mimesis?', *From Medieval to Modern in the Islamic World*, Chicago, on-line at http://humanities.uchicago.edu/orgs/institute/sawyer/archive/islam/senem.html.
34 See M.F. Köprülü, 'Ahmedi', *İslam Ansiklopedisi* (Istanbul 1943-49), vol. 1.
35 See Kritovoulos, *History of Mehmed the Conqueror*, trans. Charles Rigg (Princeton 1954); Julian Raby, 'Mehmed the Conqueror's Greek Scriptorium', *Dumbarton Oaks Papers*, 37 (1983), pp. 15–34.
36 Halil Inalcik and Rhoads Murphy, *The History of Mehmed the Conqueror by Tursun Beg* (Minneapolis 1978).
37 Güner İnal, 'The Influence of the Kazvīn Style on Ottoman Miniature Painting', *Fifth International Congress of Turkish Art*, ed. Geza Feher (Budapest 1975), p. 461.
38 See Ernst Grube, 'Four pages from a Turkish 16th century *Shahnamah* in the collection of the Metropolitan Museum of Art', *Beiträge zur Kunstgeschichte Asiens / In memoriam Ernst Dietz*, ed. Oktay Aslanapa (Istanbul 1963).
39 See Lale Uluç, 'The Majalis al-'Ushshaq: Written in Herat, Copied in Shiraz, Read in Istanbul', *M. Uğur Derman 65 Yaş Armağanı/65th Birthday Festschrift*, ed. Irvin C. Schick (Istanbul 2000), pp. 569–603.
40 İnal 1975, p. 460.
41 Edwin Binney, 3rd, *Turkish Treasure from the Collection of Edwin Binney, 3rd* (Portland 1979), esp. nos. 16, 19, 20, 37, 41, 42.
42 Topkapı Saray Müzesi, H. 1487, f. 175; illustrated in Stchoukine 1971, pl. XLIII.
43 British Library, I.O. Islamic 966, f. 189r. See B.W. Robinson, *Persian Paintings in the India Office Library* (London 1976), pp. 196–207.
44 A digital image of the colophon can be found on the *Shahnama Project* website at http://shahnama.caret.cam.ac.uk.
45 Topkapı Saray Müzesi, H. 1490, f. 59; illustrated in Stchoukine 1971, pl. XLVI.
46 Unfortunately I have not been able to see an image of this painting, but am once again grateful to Karin Rührdanz for providing me with this piece of information.
47 Topkapı Saray Müzesi, H. 2149, f. 25v; illustrated in Stchoukine 1971, pl. XLII. The other manuscript is a truncated *Shahnama* at Sam Fogg, no. 6468.
48 Berlin, Staatsbibliothek zu Berlin, Preussicher Kulturbesitz, Orientabteliung, Diez A fol. 1. This manuscript can also be viewed on the *Shahnama Project* website.
49 Illustrated in Robinson 1976, p. 110, pl. 18i.
50 Los Angeles County Museum, M. 85.237, ex-collection of Edwin Binney, 3rd, cat. no. 32b; illustrated in Binney 1979, p. 59.
51 Worcester Art Museum, Worcester, Mass, inv. 1935.16; Milstein *et al.* 1999, p. 50, illustrated fig. 68.
52 Eleanor Sims, with contribution from Tim Stanley, 'The illustrations of Baghdad 282 in the Topkapı Sarayı Library in Istanbul', in *Cairo to Kabul, Afghan and Islamic Studies presented to Ralph Pinder-Wilson*, ed. Warwick Ball and Leonard Harrow (London 2002), pp. 222–27.
53 Jerusalem, Israel Museum, inv. 539.69; illustrated in Rachel Milstein, *Miniature Painting in Ottoman Baghdad* (Costa Mesa 1990), pl. XIII. It has been drawn to my attention that Firuza Abdullaeva dealt with this iconographic borrowing, among other subjects, in an unpublished paper entitled 'The Divine and Demonic in *Shahnama* Imagery' given at the Fifth European Conference of Iranian Studies, Ravenna, on 10 October 2003.
54 Rührdanz 1997, pp. 127–28.
55 Topkapı Saray Müzesi, H. 1116, f. 14v; illustrated in Stchoukine 1971, pl. VII.
56 See M.F. Köprülü, 'Firdevsi', in *İslam Ansiklopedisi* (Istanbul 1945–48), vol. 4, *s.v.*
57 Bibliothèque nationale, suppl. Turc. 1088, ff. 9v, 20v; illustrated in Stchoukine 1971, pls. LXXXVIII, LXXXIX.
58 Topkapı Saray Müzesi, H. 1523.
59 Türk ve İslam Eserleri Müzesi, no. 1973; illustrated in *Turks, a Journey of a Thousand Years*, exh. cat., Royal Academy of Arts, London, ed. David Roxburgh (London 2005), p. 340, no. 310; Topkapı Saray Müzesi, H. 1523 and 1524; see Stchoukine 1971, p. 76, no. 45.

Bibliography

Edwin Binney, 3rd, *Turkish Treasures from the Collection of Edwin Binney, 3rd* (Portland 1979)

Sheila R. Canby, *The Golden Age of Persian Art, 1501–1722* (London 1999)

Colnaghi's, *Persian and Mughal Art* (London 1976)

L.T. Giuzalian and M.M. Diakonov, *Rukopisi Shah-name v Leningradskih Sobraniiah* (Leningrad 1934)

F. Sinem Eryilmaz, 'The Official Ottoman Shehname: An Instance of Cultural Mimesis?', *From Medieval to Modern in the Islamic World*, Chicago, online at http://humanities.uchicago.edu/orgs/institute/sawyer/archive/islam/senem.html

Oleg Grabar and Sheila Blair, *Epic Images and Contemporary History: The Illustrations of the Great Mongol Shahnama* (Chicago 1980)

Ernst Grube, 'Four pages from a Turkish 16th century *Shahnamah* in the collection of the Metropolitan Museum of Art', in *Beiträge zur Kunstgeschichte Asiens / In memoriam Ernst Dietz*, ed. Oktay Aslanapa (Istanbul 1963)

Güner İnal, 'The Influence of the Kazvīn Style on Ottoman Miniature Painting', *Fifth International Congress of Turkish Art*, ed. Geza Feher (Budapest 1975)

Halil Inalcik and Rhoads Murphy, *The History of Mehmed the Conqueror by Tursun Beg* (Minneapolis 1978)

M.F. Köprülü, 'Firdevsi', *İslam Ansiklopedisi* (Istanbul 1945–48), vol. 4

M.F. Köprülü, 'Ahmedi', *İslam Ansiklopedisi* (Istanbul 1943–49), vol. 1

Kritovoulos, *History of Mehmed the Conqueror*, trans. Charles Rigg (Princeton 1954)

Rachel Milstein, *Miniature Painting in Ottoman Baghdad* (Costa Mesa 1990)

Rachel Milstein, Karin Rührdanz, Barbara Schmitz, *Stories of the Prophets* (Costa Mesa 1999)

Mirza Muhammad Qazvini, 'Muqaddima-yi qadim-i *Shahnama*', in *Hazara-yi Firdausi* (Tehran 1322/1944)

Julian Raby, 'Mehmed the Conqueror's Greek Scriptorium', *Dumbarton Oaks Papers*, 37 (1983)

B.W. Robinson, *Persian Paintings in the India Office Library* (London 1976)

B.W. Robinson, "Ali Asghar, Court Painter', *Iran*, 26 (1988)

J.M. Rogers and R.M. Ward, *Süleyman the Magnificent* (London 1988)

Karin Rührdanz, "About a Group of Truncated *Shahnamas*: A Case Study in the Commercial Production of Illustrated Manuscripts in the Second Part of the Sixteenth Century", *Muqarnas*, 14 (1997)

Marianna Shreve Simpson, *Sultan Ibrahim Mirza's 'Haft Awrang'* (Washington, D.C. 1997)

Eleanor Sims, with contribution from Tim Stanley, 'The illustrations of Baghdad 282 in the Topkapı Sarayı Library in Istanbul', in *Cairo to Kabul, Afghan and Islamic Studies presented to Ralph Pinder-Wilson*, ed. Warwick Ball and Leonard Harrow (London 2002)

Sotheby's, London, *Catalogue of Important Oriental Manuscripts and Miniatures: The Property of the Hagop Kevorkian Fund*, 7 April 1975

Ivan Stchoukine, *La Peinture Turque, IIième Partie* (Paris 1971)

Lale Uluç, 'The Majalis al-'Ushshaq: Written in Herat, Copied in Shiraz, Read in Istanbul', *M. Uğur Derman 65 Yaş Armağanı/65th Birthday Festschrift*, ed. Irvin C. Schick (Istanbul 2000)

Anthony Welch, *Artists for the Shah* (New Haven and London 1976)

Christine Woodhead, 'An experiment in official historiography: the post of Şehnameci in the Ottoman empire, c. 1555–1605', *Wiener Zeitschrift für die Kunde des Morgenlandes*, 75 (1983)

Acknowledgements

This publication would not have been possible without the generosity of Manijeh Bayani, Charles Melville and Karin Rührdanz, who were all unstinting in sharing their time and expertise. I am also extremely grateful to Sheila Canby, Marcus Fraser, Helen Loveday, Nahla Nassar, Basil Robinson, Nabil Saidi and Eleanor Sims for their help in unravelling the complex history of the Eckstein *Shahnama*. Needless to say, any errors are entirely my own.

Illustrations copyright: © The British Library Board, London, I.O. Islamic 966. f. 189r, p. 55; © The Trustees of the Chester Beatty Library Dublin, CBL Per. 256.03, p. 41; © Freer Gallery of Art, Smithsonian Institution, Washington, D.C., Purchase, F1946.12, folio 110 verso (detail), p. 24; Israel Museum, Jerusalem, Bequest of Y. Dawud, London, 538.69, Photo © Israel Museum, Jerusalem, p. 60; © Nasser D. Khalili Collection, London, pp. 48, 49; Edwin Binney, 3rd, Collection of Turkish Art at the Los Angeles County Museum of Art, photograph © 2005 Museum Associates/LACMA, p. 59; Staatsbibliothek zu Berlin, © bpk / Staatsbibliothek zu Berlin – Orientabteilung, pp. 38, 58

Colophon

Front cover: Detail of *Salm and Tur murder Iraj*, no. 4, f. 29v
Back cover: *Akvan Div flings Rustam into the sea*, no. 18, f. 250v
Half title: Detail of *Akvan Div flings Rustam into the sea*, no. 18, f. 250v
Title page: Detail from the illuminated frontispiece, f. 1v–2r
Page 4: Detail from *Sam kills the wizard Zand*, no. 5, f. 72r

Photography: Matt Pia

Design: Roger Davies
daviesdesign@onetel.com

Produced by
Paul Holberton publishing
37 Snowsfields, London SE1 3SU
www.paul-holberton.net

Printed in Italy by Graphic Studio, Bussolengo, Verona

ISBN 0-9549014-5-2
Copyright © 2005 Sam Fogg

Distributed in Europe by Paul Holberton publishing, and in the United States and Canada for Paul Holberton publishing by University of Washington Press